Marriage

Gurpreet K

methuen | drama

LONDON • NEW YORK • OXFORD • NEW DELHI • SYDNEY

METHUEN DRAMA
Bloomsbury Publishing Plc, 50 Bedford Square, London, WC1B 3DP, UK
Bloomsbury Publishing Inc, 1359 Broadway, 12th Floor, New York, NY 10018,
USA
Bloomsbury Publishing Ireland, 29 Earlsfort Terrace, Dublin 2,
D02 AY28, Ireland

BLOOMSBURY, METHUEN DRAMA and the Methuen
Drama logo are trademarks of Bloomsbury Publishing Plc.

First published in Great Britain 2025

Cover design by FEAST

Bloomsbury Publishing Plc does not have any control over, or responsibility
for, any third-party websites referred to or in this book. All internet addresses
given in this book were correct at the time of going to press. The author and
publisher regret any inconvenience caused if addresses have changed or sites
have ceased to exist, but can accept no responsibility for any such changes.

No rights in incidental music or songs contained in the work are hereby
granted and performance rights for any performance/presentation
whatsoever must be obtained from the respective copyright owners.

All rights whatsoever in this play are strictly reserved and application
for performance etc. should be made before rehearsals begin to 42 M&P,
Palladium House, 7th Floor, 1–4 Argyll Street, London, W1F 7TA and
The Wylie Agency, 17 Bedford Square, London WC1B 3JA.

No performance may be given unless a licence has been obtained.

A catalogue record for this book is available from the British Library.

Library of Congress Control Number: 2025937221

ISBN: PB: 978-1-3505-8476-1
ePDF: 978-1-3505-8477-8
eBook: 978-1-3505-8478-5

Series: Modern Plays

Typeset by Mark Heslington Ltd, Scarborough, North Yorkshire
Printed and bound in Great Britain

For product safety related questions contact
productsafety@bloomsbury.com.

To find out more about our authors and books visit
www.bloomsbury.com and sign up for our newsletters.

This version of *Marriage Material* was first performed at the Lyric Hammersmith Theatre, London on 22 May 2025 with the following cast:

Cast

Jim / Bill / Tommy	**Tommy Belshaw**
Mr Bains / Arjan	**Jaz Singh Deol**
Surinder	**Anoushka Deshmukh**
Miss Flanagan / Claire / Reporter	**Celeste Dodwell**
Mrs Bains	**Avita Jay**
Kamaljit	**Kiran Landa**
Tanvir / Ranjit	**Omar Malik**
Dhanda	**Irfan Shamji**

Creative and Production Team

Written by **Gurpreet Kaur Bhatti**
Adapted from the book by **Sathnam Sanghera**
Directed by **Iqbal Khan**
Set & Costume Design by **Good Teeth**
Lighting Design by **Simeon Miller**
Composition & Sound Design by **Holly Khan**
Movement Direction by **Anjali Mehra**
Casting by **Jatinder Chera**
Associate Sound Design by **Anna Wood**
Associate Movement Direction by **Rakhee Sharma**
Voice & Dialect Coach **Gurkiran Kaur**
Fight & Intimacy Direction by **Dani Mac**
Assistant Director **Harper K Hefferon**

Company Stage Manager **Claire Bryan**
Deputy Stage Manager **Georgia Rose**
Assistant Stage Manager **Sarah Back**

Production Manager **Lil Dickson**
WHAM Supervisor **Sophia Khan**
WHAM Head of Department **Christina Semertzaki**
Lighting Programmer **Dan Miller**
Lighting Operator **Alistair Warr**
Sound Operator **Dan Ronayne / Scott Bradley**
Fly Person **Tom McCreadie / Will Collins**

Stage Crew **Charlotte Gregory**
Wardrobe Assistant **Lola Kezunovic**
Costume Consultant **Meghana Shah**

Costume Supervision & Making by **Lyric Costume Department**
Turbans by **Sukhvinder Singh Bamrah**
Set Built by **Liverpool Scenic Workshop**
Lighting equipment supplied by **White Light**

Audio Description **Ruth James & Willie Elliot**
Open Captioning **Miranda Yates**
BSL Interpretation **Theatresign**

PR **Bread & Butter PR**
Rehearsal & production photography by **Helen Murray**
Poster image design by **FEAST Creative**
Poster image photography by **Rich Southgate**
Programme design by **Hannah Yates**

Gurpreet Kaur Bhatti writes for stage, screen and radio.

Her first play *Behsharam* broke box office records at Soho/
Birmingham Rep. Her second play Behzti was sensationally closed
after protests and won the Susan Smith Blackburn Prize. It went
on to do sell-out tours in France and Belgium. Other credits
include *Scenes from Lost Mothers*, *Clean Break*; *A Kind of People*, Royal
Court Downstairs; *Khandan*, Royal Court Upstairs/Birmingham
Rep; *Behud*, Soho/Coventry Belgrade; *Silence*, Donmar Warehouse;
846, Stratford East; *Elephant*, Birmingham Rep; *Dishoom*, Rifco/
Watford Palace Theatre; *Fourteen*, Watford Palace Theatre; the
feature film *Everywhere And Nowhere*; *DCI Stone*, Radio 4; *Londonee*,
Rich Mix; *Dead Meat*, Channel 4; *The Archers*, Radio 4; *EastEnders*,
BBC and *An Enemy Of The People*, BBC World Service.

Her plays are published by Methuen.

ABOUT THE LYRIC

The Lyric Hammersmith Theatre produces bold and relevant world-class theatre from the heart of Hammersmith, the theatre's home for 130 years.

Under the leadership of its joint CEOs, Artistic Director Rachel O'Riordan and Executive Director Amy Belson, it is committed to being vital to, and representative of, the local community. A major force in London and UK theatre, the Lyric produces adventurous and acclaimed theatrical work that tells the stories that matter.

The Lyric is unique in its combined role as a local theatre serving its community and major national producing house, with a pioneering approach to supporting young people through and into theatre. At the core of our mission and values are the people of West London, who are vital to our work as a theatre. We are committed to working with local partners to create a cultural and creative community that brings people together, attracts visitors and supports the local economy. We bring genuinely eclectic and bold programming to West London. At the heart of programming is our desire to re-lens familiar plays that speak directly to specific communities, and a passion to welcome and engage new audiences. The Lyric Hammersmith Theatre has a national reputation for ground-breaking work to develop and nurture the next generation of talent, providing opportunities for young people to discover the power of creativity and to experience the life changing impact of theatre.

We are the creative heart of Hammersmith, proud of our history and ambitious for our future.

STAFF LIST

Executive Team
Artistic Director
Rachel O'Riordan
Executive Director
Amy Belson
Assistant to the Directors
Megan Gates

Artistic Associates
Good Teeth

Tanika Gupta
Nina Steiger

Artistic Team
Associate Director
Nicholai La Barrie

Resident Assistant Director
2024–25
Birkbeck Placement
Harper K. Hefferon

Producing Team
Director of Producing &
Planning
Chris James
Producer
Kate Baiden
Production Coordinator
Myles Sinclair
Trainee Producer
Layla Chowdhury

Young Lyric Team
Director of Young Lyric
Rob Lehmann
Education Producer
Natalie Jim
Inclusion Producer
Adrian Gardner
Talent Development Producer
Annabelle Sami
REWIND Producer
Hannah Desai
Outreach & Partnerships
Producer
Alessandra Zavagno

Young Lyric Hosts
Lanikai Krishnadasan Torrens
Daniela Lucinda Santos
Chiquita Delisser
Ricardo Ferreira
Amy Whitrod Brown

Development Team
Director of Development
Zosha Nash
Development Manager
Francesca Mirabile
130 Fundraising Campaign
Director
Lyndel Harrison
Development Officer
Lauryn Thomas

Communications & Sales Team
Director of Communications &
Sales
Grace Organ
Head of Campaigns
Sophie Blacklaw (Maternity
leave)
Box Office Manager
Nathan Rumney
Marketing Manager
Millie Whittam
Press & Marketing Assistant
Mutiat Akamo

**Box Office Assistant (Part-
Time)**
Chanel Fernandes

Box Office Assistants (Casual)
Anna Jones
Charlotte Keily
Ellie Bibby
Elliot Aitken
Emer Halton-O'Mahony
Farshid Rokey
Genevieve Sabherwal
Georgina Brown
James Douglas-Quarcoopome
lydia luke
Mackenzie Larsen
Mara Simão
Talia Kracauer

Finance & Resources Team
Interim Director of Finance
Kim Grant
Financial Controller
Charlotte Lines
Accounts and Payroll Co-
Ordinator
Lesley Williams
Finance Officer
Kunle Sanni

HR Business Partner
Beverley Dash
Administration Manager
Meghana Shah
Head of Building & Facilities
Brian Elvins
Facilities Manager
Hannah Victory
Maintenance Assistant
Ross Aylward-Tarten
Security Supervisor
Jean-Baptiste Maizeroi
Duty Security
Ilias Sufi
Sam Thompson
Housekeeping Team
Bright Gyau
Feni Wilson
Abdul-Hak Laaraj
Dipesh Sinchuri
Ivan Velinov
Nnamdi Ernest Ugorji
Samuel Anan

Production Team
Head of Production
Seamus Benson
Company Stage Manager
Claire Bryan
Deputy Head of Production
Elizabeth Dickson
Head of Stage
Will Collins
Head of Lighting
Dan Miller
Head of Sound & Video
Daniel Ronayne
Head of Costume
Harry Whitham
Studio & Events
Technical Manager
George Ogilvie

Stage Deputy
Tom McCreadie
Sound Deputy
Scott Bradley
Costume Deputy
Kyle Maenz

Commercial Team
Commercial Director
Paul Gallagher
Bars & Catering Manager
Gareth Chalmers
Events & Hires Manager
Tim Jones
Head Bars & Catering
Supervisor
Viktor Velkovski
Hires & Bookings Assistant
Ashley Quagraine-McVay
Visitor Experience Manager
Luke Vogel
Visitor Experience Co-ordinator
Bronya Doyle
Senior Duty Manager
Stephanie Dawes
Casual Duty Managers
Hana Jennings
Emma Price
Raquel Taveira-Marques
Visitor Experience Supervisors
Ellie Bibby
Wesley Bozonga
Beth Calvert Lee
Mackenzie Larsen
Ashley Quagraine-McVay
Visitor Experience Assistants
Adele Barnes
Hebe Cooke
Matthew Cowan
Hannah Crosby
Aaron Devine
James Douglas-Quarcoopome

ABOUT THE REP

Birmingham Rep has been at the forefront of theatre in the UK for over 100 years. The Rep has an unparalleled pioneering history and is the only producing theatre in the UK's second city. It is the oldest building-based theatre company in the UK, and the forerunner of both the RSC and the National Theatre.

The Rep's mission is to create artistically ambitious, world-class theatre for everyone. The commissioning and production of new work lies at the core of The Rep's programme, and over the last fifteen years the company has produced more than 130 new plays.

The Rep's acclaimed learning and outreach programme is one of the largest and most diverse of any arts organisation in the country. The Rep has nurtured new talent throughout its history – from Laurence Olivier and Peter Brook to its modern-day youth theatre, and the ground-breaking Rep Foundry theatre-makers' programme, it has offered opportunity and training for thousands of early career writers, directors and artists.

2025 Rep highlights include a sold-out new production of Khaled Hosseini's *A Thousand Splendid Suns* co-produced with Leeds Playhouse and Nottingham Playhouse; Sathnam Sanghera's *Marriage Material* adapted for stage by Gurpreet Kaur Bhatti co-produced with Lyric Hammersmith and the world premiere of *Sherlock Holmes and the 12 Days of Christmas* written by Humphry Ker and David Reed with original songs by Tim Rice and Andrew Lloyd Webber.

Many of The Rep's productions go on to have lives beyond Birmingham. The theatre's long-running production of *The Snowman* celebrated its thirtieth anniversary, alongside its forthcoming twenty-seventh consecutive season at London's Peacock Theatre. Since 2021, other Rep tours and transfers have included *A Thousand Splendid Suns*, *Community*, *Of Mice and Men*, *Idiots Assemble: Spitting Image the Musical*, *The Way Old Friends Do*, *The Play What I Wrote*, *Animal Farm* and *East is East*.

Joe Murphy became Artistic Director of The Rep in March 2025, Joe's inaugural season will be announced in September 2025.

STAFF LIST

Wardrobe Assistants
Bethany Edgar
Leanne Taylor Richards

Head of Sound & Video
Jonathan Pearce

Deputy Head of Sound & Video
Will Gilbert

Senior Sound & Video Technician
Harry Barlow

Head of Lighting
Alex Bosworth

Senior Lighting Technician
Joe Ralph

Lightning Technicians
Joseph Stairs

Head of Stage
Rosie Williams

Deputy Head of Stage
Malik Awajan

Directors of Audiences & Media
Sarah Jervis-Hill
Erin McDonald

Head of Marketing
Tim Hession

Marketing Manager
Craig Russell

Marketing Assistants
Kirstie Ewer
Lisa Varey

Head of Communications
Daniel Hicklin

Communications Assistant
Aaliyah Collins

Sales & Ticketing Managers
Hannah Kelly
Sarah Walker

Assistant Sales & Ticketing Manager
Dale Johnson

Sales & Ticketing Assistants
Dan Hagley
Ruth Holder
Olivia Linley
Ben Mitchell
Muhibb Nazir
Steven Rostance

Director of Fundraising
Sarah Cranmer

Fundraising Officers
Mahnoor Haq
Richard Wood

Head of Governance
Zoe Westwood

Director of People
Sukhi Kaur Baden

HR Manager
Tracey Wainwright

HR Officer
Jenny Coombs

Finance Director
Irina Gorbunowa

Senior Finance Officers
June Richards
Lyndsey Sturch

Finance Officer
Swapna Kaithi

Trainee Management Accountant
Tessa Jowitt

Senior Payroll Officer
Claire Monk

Head of Education
Becky Reidy

Head of Young Rep
Becky Deeks

Creative Learning Administrator
Rosalie Smith

Senior Drama Practitioner
Robert Beck

Drama Practitioners
William Costello
Jasmin Hylton

Facilities & Operations Director
Hamid Ghadry

Facilities & Operations Manager
Nigel Cairns

Building Maintenance Technician
Leon Gatenby

Security Concierges
Kamran Ali
Darren Holbrook
Mohamed Ibrahim
Peter Moore
Tyler Phillips

Stage Door Receptionists
Jonathan Arnold
Shannon James
Kimberley Musa

Alexander Oakes
Imaani Phillips

Housekeeping Supervisor
Jane Browning

Housekeeping Assistants
Marcus Elliman
Guy Essom
Liam Farrell
Fay Gayle
Christine Hoxha
Tracey O'Dell
Amy Proctor
Beverley Shale
Rajat Sthapit

Customer Experience Manager
Jade Senior

Duty Managers
Susanne Barton
Aaron Kendell
Matty Sanders
Sarah Walker

Café & Bar Manager
Sam Richardson

Café & Bar Supervisors
Arrahnne Allen
Stephanie Carter

UVB Managing Director
Suzanna Reid Barreiro da Silva

UVB Business Development Manager
Claire Sutton

UVB Sales & Events Executive
Jordan Davidson

UVB Sales & Events Coordinators
Leah Kenny-Erdington
Kayleigh Palmer

UVB General Manager
Rory Shannon

UVB Operations Manager
Kate Edwards

UVB Food & Beverage Manager
Adam Finney

UVB Head Chef
Lee Barnett

UVB Back of House Supervisor
Christopher Gunn

UVB Hospitality Managers
Layo Oladejo
Jack Broad
Callum Connolly

UVB Hospitality Team Members
Ipshita Jaiswal
Ismael Mahate

UVB Customer Experience Coordinator
Vera Neves

UVB Events & Technical Managers
Jabari Douglas
Jack Shaw

Marriage Material

For Uma and Mali, with so much love

THANKS TO –

Rachel O'Riordan for her courage
and commitment to this story

The teams at the Lyric Hammersmith and the
Birmingham Rep for their dedication and hard work

Roxana Silbert and Tessa Walker,
without whom there would be no play

Cathy King and Alex Bloch for everything as always

Iqbal Khan for his brilliant eye

and Sathnam Sanghera for his generosity and trust

Characters

Mr Bains/Arjan, *South Asian male*
Mrs Bains, *South Asian female*
Dhanda, *South Asian male*
Tanvir/Ranjit, *South Asian male*
Surinder, *South Asian female*
Kamaljit, *South Asian female*
Jim/Bill/Tommy, *White male*
Miss Flanagan/Reporter/Claire, *White female*

Locations

Past
Bains' Living Area
Shop
Street
Restaurant
Bedsit

Present
Bains' Living Area
Shop
Shed
Street
Club
Flat
Lobby
Park
Wedding Hall

Prologue

1960s. Midlands. **Bains'** *living area – the Baithak – the area between the shop front and the kitchen. The shop counter is visible at one side, as is the kitchen on the other side, there should be a flow of activity between the different spaces. Cardboard boxes, filled with stock, are piled high.* **Mrs Bains** *kneels on the floor, pricing bars of soap.* **Mr Bains** *sits on a chair.* **Dhanda** *is on a low stool, both men are drinking tea.*

Dhanda   What do you expect? From a gora [*white man*]?

Mr Bains   Bill was my friend.

Dhanda   No, no, no! They are not our friends, Birji. My Charna came home from school crying because one of his 'friends' tried to cut off his topknot with a pen knife.

He turns to **Mrs Bains**.

Dhanda   Remember what I said to you, Bhanji, about Bill.

Mrs Bains   You say lots of things, Prahji.

Dhanda (*not listening/points towards shop*)   He sat there eating humbugs, then once every hour he would take the newspaper into the toilet and I would be left on the counter. That kutha [*dog*] would leave the door open. The smell, Birji, the smell! These goreh do not smell like other humans. (*A beat.*) I knew he was lazy, a bad egg. But I never suspected he was rotten. Stealing! From you! After all you did for him. I blame myself.

Mr Bains   You?

Dhanda   You pay me to be your eyes, Birji. How could I let him deceive me?

Mrs Bains   Bill was too sneaky.

Mr Bains   Charging always full price but putting only half the money in the till.

Mrs Bains   And he was taking food, mainly custard creams and tinned peaches. Hiding them down his jean and under his bobble hat.

Dhanda   Kutha [*Dog*] . . . Haramjadah [*Bastard*] . . . Bhenjot [*Sisterfucker*]! Soon he will be getting into bed with Enoch. Mark my words, that one is getting ready to chuck a brick through your window.

Mrs Bains   Bill wouldn't.

Tanvir *enters carrying a rack made out of wood.*

Tanvir   Uncle, I finished!

He holds a wooden rack, alongside bread, paper and string.

Tanvir   For the bread.

Mr Bains   Nice work, Tanvir.

Tanvir   Thank you, Uncle. And I made space for the brown paper and string. You take the bread, then the paper . . .

He tries to show them but keeps messing up. **Mrs Bains** *gets up and takes the items from him.*

Mrs Bains (*demonstrates*)   You take the bread, then the paper and tie it up in a bow.

Tanvir   That's right!

Mrs Bains   A loaf wrapped in brown paper and tied with string always looks fresh.

Tanvir   Extremely fresh!

Dhanda (*indicating rack*)   I could have bought you one of these from the market?

Tanvir   Only cheapie people purchase essential hardware from the market. I made this with my bare hands.

He proudly hands it to **Mr Bains**.

Tanvir   Built to last, like the London Bridge!

As **Mr Bains** *examines it, the structure immediately falls apart. They all stare at it.* **Tanvir** *tries to put it back together.*

Dhanda (*to* **Tanvir**)   You know Bill was a thief?

Mr Bains *has a coughing fit.*

Tanvir   That fellow is why Uncle's lungs are running out of breath.

Dhanda   The police must be throwing away the key, heh Birji?

Mrs Bains   The police let him go.

Dhanda   I will inform our Association.

Dhanda *gets up to leave.*

Dhanda   They listen to me. You deserve justice.

Mr Bains   In this des [*country*]? Men like us?

Dhanda   If we organise ourselves correctly, these goreh will realise we are here to stay.

Mr Bains   Those Association idiots can't do nothing.

Dhanda   Let us see. (*Observes* **Tanvir** *trying to fix the broken rack.*) Leave that, Tanvir. I will buy you a new one, Birji. From the market.

He heads out.

Mr Bains   Patwant! Don't you want my blessing?

Dhanda *stops.* **Mr Bains** *turns to the others.*

Mr Bains   Patwant is opening a shop.

Mrs Bains   Kee [*what*]?

Mr Bains   Number 78 Victoria Road. The old butcher has a bad hip and his son wants to be a pop star, so they need someone to rent the lease. Patwant has been saving his pennies.

Dhanda (*A beat*)   You have been my everything, Birji. Father, mother, brother. You took in a poor boy and showed him how to be a man. I will never compete with you.

Mrs Bains   So why are you opening a shop?

Dhanda   I am planning to sell different stock. Pandeh [*dishes*], plugs, beer, whisky and the suchlike.

Mrs Bains   They say you make more money from beer than from white loaves and pear drops.

Dhanda   Bhanji, sharab is a hard business! The drunks are your best friends during the day but at closing time they pull down their trousers, show you their bottoms and call you Paki.

Dhanda *puts his hands together, half pleading, half apologetic to* **Mr Bains**.

Dhanda   Your blessing will give me and my missus hope for a life.

Mr Bains   You talk too much and too loudly, Patwant. But you are a hard worker and you have warmed my blood in this cold country. (*A beat.*) Give me your first bottle of Johnnie Walker when you open.

Dhanda *touches* **Mr Bains**'s *feet*.

Dhanda   When I look at my Charna, I wish I could give you half of my boy.

Mrs Bains   There are two children already under this roof!

Dhanda   Kismet has burdened you badly, Birji, by surrounding you with females. You will see, this shop will be your son.

Surinder *can be seen doing schoolwork in the shop.* **Kamaljit** *is cooking in the kitchen.*

Dhanda (*indicates shop*)   It will make your fortune. And then your daughters will marry great men and have sons who will have more sons. Outside, these goreh might spit at our faces, but inside these walls, we will be kings of England. And we will make this place our place. These goreh, we will show them. We will show them!

A movement section showing **Mr Bains***'s decline. He goes from his seat to lying on a makeshift bed.*

Act One

Scene One

Years later. The Baithak has been smartened up, with a telephone in the corner. **Tanvir** *is sweeping the kitchen and* **Mrs Bains** *is busy in the shop.* **Mr Bains** *lies on the makeshift bed.* **Kamaljit** *feeds him with a spoon.* **Surinder** *approaches with a stainless steel beaker of water.*

Kamaljit Well done, Daddy.

Surinder He's not a baby, Kamaljit!

The two girls sit with him, each holding one of his hands lovingly.

Mr Bains I'm going to race you in the park, Surinder. And I'm going to beat you.

Mr Bains *holds his hand out for the water.* **Surinder** *helps him drink.*

Mr Bains My boy. My good boy.

Surinder I'm a girl.

Kamaljit Stop upsetting him!

Mr Bains One day he will be Prime Minister.

Surinder And I'll get a short back and sides.

Kamaljit You wash your mouth out!

Mr Bains *and* **Surinder** *laugh.*

Mr Bains Be quiet, Kamaljit, we are just having the fun. (*A beat.*) I sleep now.

He shuts his eyes.

Surinder Later we'll go to the park, Daddy.

They watch him fall asleep.

But you'll never catch me.

She stands up, wheels **Mr Bains'** *bed towards the shop area.*

Kamaljit   What are you doing?

Surinder   Moving him closer to the till, he likes to sniff the pound notes.

She finds a magazine, positions a stool in the centre of the room. Puts newspaper down on the floor. **Tanvir** *enters.*

Tanvir   Ready?

Surinder   Almost.

He sits on the stool. **Surinder** *finds a page in a magazine. Takes out scissors.*

Kamaljit   I'm telling Mum.

Surinder   She doesn't care.

Kamaljit   Try cutting yours and see.

Surinder *brandishes the scissors.* **Kamaljit** *takes the dishes into the kitchen, tidies up.*

Surinder   Once I've finished with you, people are gonna think you're that Tony Curtis.

Tanvir   You said Shashi Kapoor.

Surinder   You won't be you any more, that's the point.

Kamaljit   Thought you were growing it, Tanvir.

Tanvir   I can always grow it again after I've had it cut.

Surinder   Exactly! We're not in the village now, Kamaljit. There are people in Wolverhampton with colour tellies.

She dances around the space.

Kamaljit   You should be fasting today, not dancing around like you're on Top of the Pops.

Surinder   Wish I was!

She reads the magazine.

Kamaljit   Where's your sharam [*shame*]?

Surinder   Forgot the towel.

She rushes out. **Tanvir** *gets up, he and* **Kamaljit** *behold one another nervously. Draw closer to one another.*

Kamaljit   Are you really going to have it done like Shashi Kapoor?

Tanvir   Er . . . well . . . I want to do whatever I can to . . . improve myself. (*A beat.*) What do you think?

They tentatively move closer and closer when **Surinder** *comes back. They hurriedly part.* **Tanvir** *sits back down and* **Surinder** *puts a towel round his shoulders and checks the magazine.*

Surinder (*reads*)   Make sectional partings across the head. And cut from the nape.

Kamaljit   I could do it.

Surinder   What do you know about fashion?

She starts cutting his hair.

Kamaljit   I can follow instructions!

Surinder   You're not brave enough to touch another human.

Kamaljit   Who wipes Dad every morning?

Surinder   I'm not talking about Dad.

Mrs Bains *enters carrying boxes. She puts them down, starts pricing.*

Mrs Bains   The driver delivered two boxes of marrowfat peas by mistake.

Surinder   How can they actually eat those?

Mrs Bains   They have different tastes. It's not for us to judge what people put in their mouths.

Tanvir   Imagine if goreh tried tandoori chicken.

They all laugh.

Kamaljit   They never would.

Surinder (*indicating boxes*)   You should have given these back, Mum.

Mrs Bains   I asked. The kutha laughed in my face. (*To* **Surinder**.) What are you doing?

Kamaljit   Turning Tanvir into a skinhead.

Mrs Bains   You've got no sharam, Surinder.

Surinder   Miss Flanagan says, when we're not revising, we should be expanding our horizons, maybe learn a new skill.

Kamaljit   Mum, tell her to stop.

Mrs Bains   Who listens to me?

Surinder   I'm smartening him up.

Tanvir   I want to look nice, Auntie, for the customers.

Mrs Bains   The customers don't look at you, Tanvir.

She eyes **Surinder**.

Mrs Bains   Put your chunni [*scarf*] on properly, Surinder.

Surinder   But I'm not going anywhere.

Mrs Bains   Just do it.

Surinder *reluctantly rearranges her chunni.* **Mrs Bains** *turns to* **Kamaljit**.

Mrs Bains   Have you fed Daddy?

Kamaljit   Yes.

Mrs Bains   Tidied the kitchen?

Kamaljit   Yes.

Mrs Bains (*to* **Surinder**)   Once you've finished your nonsense you can goon the atta [*knead the dough*] . . .

Surinder   Mum, these next exams are my actual O-levels!

Mrs Bains   What's more important, feeding your family or feeding your brain with stupid facts that you're never going to use?

Surinder   I might use them.

Tanvir   Did the man selling the chocolate come, Auntie?

Mrs Bains   Not today.

Kamaljit   What's that?

Tanvir   A salesman's bringing a new selection of bars. They sent a letter.

Kamaljit   Do we get to taste?

Mrs Bains   No you do not!

She goes to put the boxes in the shop corner. **Surinder** *takes off her chunni.*

Surinder   Save us some, won't you, Tan?

Kamaljit   He's not supposed to.

Tanvir   Course I will.

Kamaljit   If there's one with soft mint cream in the middle, can I have it?

Tanvir   I'll make sure.

Mrs Bains *returns with more boxes. At the same time, a buoyant* **Dhanda** *bustles in from the kitchen. He has the air of a man who has become accustomed to success, he carries a small box.*

Dhanda   Bhanji!

Mrs Bains   Prahji.

Dhanda *regards* **Tanvir** *with his half-shorn hair.*

Dhanda   What is this?

Mrs Bains   Er . . . poor Tanvir has . . . fleas.

Dhanda   Hai, hai . . .

Mrs Bains   So we are disinfecting the fleabag. Aren't we, kurreeyoh [*girls*]?

Surinder   Hanji [*Yes*].

Mrs Bains   You two, clean him up and make chah for Uncle.

The girls instantly clean up around **Tanvir** *and spring into a well-oiled routine, almost like a dance where they assemble a tea tray with biscuits.* **Tanvir** *gets up,* **Dhanda** *dodges him and goes to crouch at* **Mr Bains'** *feet.* **Tanvir** *heads into the shop.*

Dhanda   How is my Birji today?

Mrs Bains   Same as usual.

The girls bring his tea.

Dhanda   When he wakes, I will tell him the football scores. You like that Georgie Best, isn't it, Birji? Oh, and I brought him some barfi.

Mrs Bains (*takes box*)   He'll enjoy this.

The girls bring in flour and dhal.

Dhanda   Soon he will be behind the counter again. Punching and kicking the paper boys when they are late for their rounds.

Surinder   No, he won't.

Awkward silence. **Kamaljit** *sorts through the dhal while* **Surinder** *kneads the dough.*

Dhanda   Such good girls you have.

Mrs Bains   Yes. Is Bhanji keeping well, Prahji?

Dhanda   My missus is heading back to India next month. My Beji [*mother*] is suffering with her toilet trouble and Sarjit will be looking after her.

Mrs Bains   What about little Charna?

Dhanda   Going with his mummy. A man can't take care of a child on his own.

Mrs Bains   Certainly not. Who will be making your roti?

Dhanda   I will be relying on the kindness of the ladies from the Gurdwara.

Mrs Bains   There will always be roti here, waiting for you, whenever you need it.

Dhanda   I shall remember that, Bhanji. But I am not here to discuss my roti . . .

Tanvir *brings in more boxes. Prices the stock.*

Surinder   Why are you here, Uncle?

Dhanda   Because Surinder, these goreh, always these goreh are trying to break the Sardar [*Sikh man*]!

Tanvir   How are they doing that?

Dhanda   They are happy for us to wear the turban when we are fighting wars for their British Empire, but now they are saying we cannot wear our religious attire when we work on the buses of Wolverhampton.

Kamaljit   That doesn't sound fair.

Dhanda   Exactly, Kamaljit beta [*dear*]. Men like me are being stripped of our human rights.

Surinder   But you don't wear a turban.

Dhanda *takes a biscuit.*

Dhanda   The point here, is the case of Sohan Singh Jolly.

Mrs Bains   That man talks too much.

Dhanda Jolly Sahib is no fool, Bhanji. The fellow lost an arm while fighting Kikuyu during the Mau Mau revolt. He has denounced Wolverhampton Transport Committee as the worst racialists in the world.

Kamaljit I reckon he's right.

Dhanda If the turban ban is not lifted, Sohan Singh Jolly has declared that he will burn himself alive on 13 April.

Mrs Bains But that's Basaikhi [*Sikh festival*].

Dhanda Quite.

Mrs Bains Are you allowed to burn yourself alive on Basaikhi?

Dhanda I'm not sure. (*A beat*.) Unfortunately that bandar [*twit*] Tommy Higginbottom is making matters worse.

Kamaljit Tommy Higginbottom who does cut and blow dries on the precinct?

Dhanda Hanji. He is threatening to burn himself alive if the committee give in to Jolly's demands. Following this, Jarman Singh Parmar, editor of the Indian Observer has vowed to also set himself on fire fifteen days after Jolly sahib. One of us will do the same every fifteen days until this racialist policy is reversed. (*A beat*.) Jolly Sahib needs us to show the citizens of Wolverhampton that we mean business. So, we, the Gurdwara committee, are planning a protest in the city centre in two weeks. Can we count on your support?

Uneasy silence.

Surinder My teacher says we should be spending as much time as possible studying.

Mrs Bains (*A beat*) We will be there for sure, Prahji.

Tanvir What about the shop?

Mrs Bains We will manage.

Surinder Someone'll have to stay with Daddy.

Kamaljit   That's true.

Surinder   I can. I'll keep an eye on the counter as well.

Dhanda   You are a young girl . . .

Surinder   I'm old enough.

Dhanda   You should not be here alone.

Surinder   Daddy's here.

Dhanda   Your father cannot protect you.

Surinder   He's not dead yet!

Suddenly **Mrs Bains** *slaps* **Surinder** *round the face.*

Mrs Bains   You don't talk to Uncle like that. (*A beat.*) She is sad because of her daddy, you understand.

Dhanda   This young one has always had spirit.

Mrs Bains   Soon she will learn.

Dhanda   You should teach her, before she gets married.

Mrs Bains   We are not planning their marriages yet.

Dhanda   I will discuss with Birji next time.

He goes to leave.

Mrs Bains   Tanvir, go and give Prahji the moolis [*horseradishes*] from the vegetable box.

Tanvir *jumps up, heads towards the shop.*

Mrs Bains   I thought perhaps Sarjit Bhanji would like to make paratheh?

Dhanda   I will ask but my missus is not the cleverest in the kitchen. Sat siri akal.

Mrs Bains   Sat siri akal.

They watch **Dhanda** *follow* **Tanvir** *into the shop. As soon as he's out of sight,* **Mrs Bains** *turns to* **Surinder,** *grabs her by the hair.*

Kamaljit   Mum, leave her please!

She shields her sister. They both fall to the floor. **Surinder**'s *hair comes loose.*

Mrs Bains   Now he will tell everyone at the Gurdwara that you are doing O-levels!

Surinder   We're not really getting married, are we?

Kamaljit   Course not.

Mrs Bains   What else do you think you're going to do?

The girls take this in. **Mrs Bains** *points at* **Surinder.**

Mrs Bains   And tonight you're doing the night shift with Daddy.

Surinder   I did it yesterday.

Mrs Bains   Well you're doing it again. And every single night this week. Until you learn not to be a stupid! Now finish the atta, I need to make Daddy's roti.

She walks into the kitchen. The girls sit in silence.

Surinder   Why does he always come round?

Kamaljit   Uncle's alright.

Surinder   You know he isn't. (*A beat.*) I just want to do well at school . . .

Kamaljit   You might be able to, if you shut your mouth.

Surinder (*A beat*)   What do you want?

Kamaljit   Me?

Surinder   There must be something. (*Indicates her heart.*) Inside . . . here.

Kamaljit (*A beat*)   Find someone special who thinks I'm special too and have a load of kids. Five or seven. A gang of us. We'd go up the high street to the shops . . . and then come home and . . . they'd play hopscotch and I'd eat black forest gateau. I saw a picture of it in a magazine. It's from Germany.

Surinder   Are you ready to get married, Kamaljit? Actually married.

Kamaljit   It's not up to us.

Surinder   Wish it was.

Kamaljit   Shut up now. Try learning to have some sharam.

She cradles her sister in her arms, starts smoothing down **Surinder**'s *hair.*

Surinder   I do try.

Kamaljit *starts to sing* Build me Up Buttercup. *They both sing together.*

Scene Two

Later that night. **Surinder** *sits with her father who lies on his bed. She massages his legs.*

Mr Bains   Newspapers?

Surinder   A handful.

Mr Bains   Bread?

Surinder   Gone.

Mr Bains   Butter?

Surinder   Sold out.

Mr Bains   More coming?

Surinder   Tanvir said first thing in the morning.

Mr Bains   Acha [*right*]. Is important to keep up stock levels. If a man has stock he will never go out of business.

Surinder   Yes, Daddy.

Mr Bains   Tanvir must learn.

Surinder   He manages to run the shop.

Mr Bains   I run my shop! You people better not bloody forget it.

Surinder   We won't.

Mr Bains   Stop doing the malash [*massage*]. You are sending too much blood into my circulation.

She gently retreats.

Surinder   There's new chocolate coming.

Mr Bains   Keep the bars away from Kamaljit. I know she steals the Creme Eggs. Stuffed a whole one in her mouth the other day. She thought I didn't see. But I did.

Surinder   That girl dreams about chocolate.

Mr Bains   She should stop. No mother-in-law wants her son's bride to have spots on her face and a fatty tummy.

Surinder (*A beat*)   What . . . do you dream about, Daddy?

Mr Bains   I don't have no dreams no more.

Surinder   Did you used to?

Mr Bains   When I was young. Your age.

Surinder   Go on.

Mr Bains   Leave the village. Come to Belayt. Start a business. Live in a castle. Drive a Mercedes Benz. Become a somebody. Have a beautiful wife to make my roti and hold my hand at night. One daughter and one son to call me Daddy.

Surinder   I call you Daddy.

Mr Bains   Did I ever tell you your grandmother left you in the sun when you were born?

Surinder   Tell me again.

Mr Bains   All the old women in the village said you don't need another girl. Leave her outside for one day and see if she lives or dies. Your mummy screamed when they took you from her arms. And you didn't stop crying for a single second. After two hours, I grabbed you, told them to stop playing games with my flesh and blood. You know, your mummy only started to love me from that day. And then . . . and then . . . we never let you go.

Surinder   I must have wanted to live.

Mr Bains   Oh yes.

Surinder   I've got dreams, Daddy.

Mr Bains   Acha?

Surinder   I'm doing well at school. Not like Kamaljit. My teacher said I should stay on, do A-levels.

Mr Bains   For what?

Surinder   If I get an education, I can learn more stuff to help with the shop. We could expand.

Mr Bains   You are telling me about my business?

Surinder   To support my family. I like working.

Mr Bains   You are a hard worker.

Surinder   I might . . . even get a job. I'd still cook and clean and everything. But I'd . . . be a somebody. (*A beat.*) What do you think?

Mr Bains   You think too much. What job you like?

Surinder   Maybe a nurse or a teacher . . .

Mr Bains (*amused*)   My daughter wants to be a somebody.

Surinder   Like you.

Mr Bains   We will find a somebody for you to marry.

Surinder   But what about . . . my life.

Mr Bains   You think this is your life?

Surinder   It's me in this body.

Mr Bains   You is my girl. What are you, thirteen, fourteen?

Surinder   Sixteen.

Mr Bains   You think the goreh will let you take one of their jobs?

Surinder   They're not all bad.

Mr Bains   I didn't say they were bad. But they will always look at you like you are different. Make you feel different.

Surinder   Thought you wanted to get away from the village.

Mr Bains   You know what the goreh did when they came to my country? Made us learn English, took our women, built their own little Belayt. They never became Indian because they thought they were better. You think I'm going to let my family be infected with English ways. Not on your bloody nelly.

Surinder   You brought us here, Daddy. What are we supposed to do?

Mr Bains   What I say!

Surinder *recoils slightly.* **Mr Bains** *feels bad.*

Mr Bains   You think I don't see the boys looking at you through the shop window. Kamaljit will be lucky to find a boy that is even breathing. You, you will be able to choose.

No response.

You want to make me happy or not?

Surinder *half nods.*

Mr Bains   My good boy.

He slowly sleeps. **Surinder** *retreats.*

Scene Three

Living area. **Kamaljit** *is tidying up.* **Tanvir** *runs in holding a radio.*

Tanvir They're playing it now.

Kamaljit Really?

He nods vigorously.

What about the shop?

Tanvir It'll only be two minutes.

The first few notes of Sugar, Sugar *play. They both start dancing clumsily but joyfully and sing along to one another. A woman,* **Miss Flanagan**, *enters. She watches them jumping around, somewhat bemused.* **Kamaljit** *notices her. Grabs the radio, turns it off. They all stare at one another.*

Kamaljit Are you?

Miss Flanagan That's right.

Kamaljit You look older.

Miss Flanagan I remember you from school. The children used to call you . . . er . . .

Kamaljit Camel Shit.

Miss Flanagan The door was open.

Tanvir Er . . . thank you for reconnecting the loose wires inside the radio, Kamaljit.

Kamaljit You're very welcome, Tanvir. I hope it works now.

Tanvir I'm sure it's perfect.

He awkwardly retreats into the shop area. **Kamaljit** *eyes* **Miss Flanagan** *nervously.*

Miss Flanagan He seems like a nice young man.

Kamaljit He's not. (*Shouts.*) Mum, come here (*in Punjabi*).

Mrs Bains *and* **Surinder** *approach from the kitchen.*

Miss Flanagan   Hello, Surinder.

Surinder   You're early, Miss.

Miss Flanagan   Good afternoon, Mrs Bains, I'm Miss Flanagan, Surinder's English teacher and head of fifth year. I sent a note saying I'd be popping round.

Surinder   She read the note.

Mrs Bains   I have a mouth! (*A beat.*) I read the note. Is she in trouble?

Miss Flanagan   No. No trouble.

Mrs Bains   Please sit. (*Nods to* **Kamaljit**.) Kamaljit, chah.

Kamaljit *hurries to the kitchen.* **Mrs Bains**, **Miss Flanagan** *and* **Surinder** *sit. Awkward silence.* **Miss Flanagan** *picks up a magazine next to her. She scans the picture of the Viking warrior on the front.*

Miss Flanagan   The Vikings! They were immigrants. From Scandinavia. People always describe them as bloodthirsty and murderous. And they did wear unusual hats and pillage churches but apparently they were excellent handymen. Nobody's all bad, are they?

Mrs Bains   Who?

Miss Flanagan   Er, the Vikings.

Surinder   It's a joke, Mum.

Mrs Bains *forces polite laughter.*

Miss Flanagan   Who are the British anyway? I mean, there are two million people living in this country who were not born here. The problem with the likes of Enoch Powell is that he has no historical awareness. Not even first year standard. Your daughter could teach him a thing or two?

Mrs Bains   Kamaljit?

Miss Flanagan   No, Surinder.

Mrs Bains   Oh.

Miss Flanagan   I don't want to embarrass you, but she is bright. Ridiculously bright.

Mrs Bains (*yells*)   Kamaljit, chah!

Kamaljit (*from kitchen*)   I'm coming!

Mrs Bains   You ever tried a samosa?

Miss Flanagan   Er . . . yes. So, I'm here . . .

Kamaljit *brings in the chah.*

Miss Flanagan   . . . to talk about Surinder.

Mrs Bains   Have a samosa. With the imli chutney.

Miss Flanagan   Oh . . . er . . . I will . . .

Mrs Bains   They are tasty. With the chutney. Homemade. By me.

Miss Flanagan   Right.

Mrs Bains   Eat!

Miss Flanagan *takes a samosa, munches it.* **Mrs Bains** *eyes her.*

Mrs Bains   You want to know the secret to making a superior samosa?

Miss Flanagan   Okay.

Mrs Bains   My secret is to fry on low gas. So the samosa cooks evenly from the inside out. Makes the pastry crispy. Not greasy. Is it crispy?

Miss Flanagan   Yes.

Mrs Bains   How crispy?

Miss Flanagan   Very.

Mrs Bains   Is it the crispiest samosa you have ever eaten?

Miss Flanagan   Possibly.

Mrs Bains   Because I am patient. With the gas. And patience is paradise, Miss Flan.

Miss Flanagan (*A beat*)   I wouldn't be surprised if she gets top grades in all her O-levels.

Mrs Bains   Who?

Miss Flanagan   Surinder.

Mrs Bains   Drink your chah. You want to know the secret to making superior chah?

Miss Flanagan   Well . . .

Mrs Bains   Put whole spices in cold water with a big spoon of tea, bring to a rolling boil and then you add the milk!

Miss Flanagan   Mrs Bains . . .

Mrs Bains   You want to know the secret to making extra superior tarka dhal?

Miss Flanagan (*firm*)   Mrs Bains, I think it would be a pity if Surinder didn't stay on at school.

Mrs Bains   Too much education makes people's brains get mixed up, they don't sleep at night and then they have to force their toilet out in the morning.

Miss Flanagan   Or they learn new ways of thinking. Do astonishing things like build bridges and skyscrapers. Surinder absorbs knowledge and turns it into something incisive and sometimes . . . extraordinary.

Mrs Bains *regards her with suspicion.*

Miss Flanagan   My parents came here from Ireland. They wanted a better life, but my mother was terrified about me going into this place that was foreign . . . she'd been spat at, had her hair pulled . . . and worse. I don't have to tell you . . . The point is . . . (*Falters.*)

Mrs Bains   What is the point, Miss Flan?

Miss Flanagan   My mother realised this better life would only come if she was brave . . . so she decided to let me go.

Mrs Bains   You want me to allow my daughter out into your world.

Miss Flanagan   Our world, Mrs Bains. And it's going to be hers.

Mrs Bains   You . . . you think my Surinder might build a bridge?

Miss Flanagan   Your daughter can do things that nobody else in her class can do.

Mrs Bains   Clever?

Miss Flanagan   Yes.

Mrs Bains (*sinking in*)   She is clever . . .

Miss Flanagan   The cleverest. But she needs someone to believe in her.

Mrs Bains   You . . .

Miss Flanagan   No, not me.

Mrs Bains *gets up.*

Mrs Bains   I have to go to the toilet.

Surinder   Mum . . .

Mrs Bains *heads out.* **Miss Flanagan** *gets up.*

Miss Flanagan   Will you consider it?

Surinder   I'm begging you, Mum. I swear I'll do whatever you say, if I can carry on . . .

Mrs Bains   Okay, okay.

Surinder *goes to hug her mother but* **Mrs Bains** *continues on.*

Mrs Bains   If you love school so much, go and get your history, chemistry blah blah books.

Surinder (*delighted*)   I will.

Mrs Bains (*going*)   And tell your teacher to eat more samoseh . . . and buy fish and chips on the way home. She is too bloody well thin.

Scene Four

Bains' *living area.* **Mr Bains** *lies on his makeshift bed.* **Surinder** *sits nearby doing her homework.* **Dhanda**, **Mrs Bains**, **Kamaljit** *and* **Tanvir** *are dressed up to the nines.*

Kamaljit *and* **Tanvir** *unfurl a long white sheet which reads –* *TURBANS BELONG ON WOLVERHAMPTON BUSES.*

Dhanda   Impressive heh, Birji. We will be thousands in the town centre. Coaches of apneh [*our people*] are arriving from Walsall, Slough, Southall.

Mr Bains   I should come and give the chairman of the Transport Committee a big fat thupurr. (*Mimes slap.*)

Mr Bains *has a bad coughing attack. The women go to him, gently stroke his shoulder.*

Tanvir   Maybe we shouldn't leave him.

Mr Bains   Him? Who is him you bhenjot [*sisterfucker*]? Don't forget you are my representatives. This family needs to have a presence on a day like this. (*To* **Dhanda**.) I let them close my shop. For one day only!

Mrs Bains (*to* **Mr Bains**)   Surinder will be with you.

Mr Bains   I don't need no girl looking after me.

Mrs Bains (*to* **Dhanda**)   She is becoming more and more devoted to her daddy.

Dhanda   Her spirit is certainly calmer. I can see she is a very simple girl nowadays.

Kamaljit   Will there be a riot, Uncle?

Dhanda   We are a peaceful people, beta [*dear*]. But if they antagonise us, we must be prepared.

Mrs Bains   Finish up in the shop Surinder. And then sit with Daddy. His dhal and roti's on the stove.

Surinder *heads into the shop.*

Dhanda   Chullo everybody!

Mrs Bains   Let me get my shawl. I will catch up.

Dhanda, **Tanvir** *and* **Kamaljit** *head out.* **Mrs Bains** *beholds her husband.*

Mrs Bains   Sure you are okay?

She finds her shawl. Pointedly picks up a book.

Mr Bains   Yes, woman. Stop fussing.

He takes the book from her hands.

Mr Bains   Who is this . . . Tess of the d'Urbervilles?

Mrs Bains   It's for Surinder's exams.

Mr Bains   She reads too many books.

Mrs Bains   Girls in this country read. Do things. School says she's intelligent, cleverest in the class. (*A beat.*) Perhaps we should give her a chance.

Mr Bains   No more school.

Mrs Bains   It's only two more years.

Mr Bains   Enough time for her to become someone who is not like us.

Mrs Bains   Why not give her a few more months of a life?

Mr Bains   A woman like you can't make a decision about my child.

Mrs Bains   Surinder has a quick brain and a spirit of iron. She can do better for herself.

Mr Bains   Better than what?

Mrs Bains   You know.

Mr Bains *takes* **Mrs Bains***'s hand.*

Mr Bains   You always dreamed big. That's why you still set me on fire.

He pulls her towards him. They kiss.

Mr Bains   I want to see Surinder's wedding.

Mrs Bains   Better not go blind then. (*A beat.*) Kamaljit is kind and she can clean but not much else. Plus she is older so she should go first.

Mr Bains   They will all want Surinder. That girl was born with some magic . . .

Mrs Bains   If she leaves, who will help me run the shop?

Mr Bains   My shop.

Mrs Bains   You know I can just decide. And you can't do nothing!

Mr Bains (*laughs*)   Woman, you love me too much to insult me.

Mrs Bains   Would it be so bad if we let her go?

Mr Bains   My girls are my izzat [*honour*]!

Mrs Bains   Your izzat doesn't wake at 4 am to get the papers ready! It doesn't make saag and keema and muttar paneer. It doesn't say nothing when the goreh shout at us to get out of their country. You sit here like a king. Order us around like servants. We take it, we do what you say. But that teacher said my daughter is special. And this chance . . . this is what I want for her.

Mr Bains   You are going to bring trouble into this house. Big trouble.

Mrs Bains   Well?

Mr Bains   When have I ever not given you what you want?

Mrs Bains *strokes his shoulder lovingly. He closes his eyes.*

Scene Five

The march. A street. A dhol plays a loud bhangra beat. And the sound of Punjabi folk music blares out. The actors advance on stage dressed as protestors holding placards. Defiant shouts can be heard over the music.

Protestors   Sikhs have rights! . . . You brought us to this country to do your dirty work! We are here to stay! . . . Shame on you, Transport Committee!

The music and shouts blend into a rendition of 'We Shall Not Be Moved', *which culminates in a climactic bellowing of 'Bole So Nihal. Sat Siri Akal'.*

A reporter takes out a microphone. Shoves it in front of **Tanvir** *and* **Kamaljit**.

Reporter   Surely when in Rome, you should do as the Romans do?

Tanvir   Thing is, we are actually in Wolverhampton.

Loud cheers. **Kamaljit** *applauds fervently.*

Reporter   Would you both describe yourselves as devout Sikhs?

Tanvir   Certainly.

Kamaljit   Absolutely.

Reporter   But you're not wearing a turban.

Tanvir   My faith is in my soul.

Kamaljit   That's lovely, Tanvir.

Reporter   Right.

Kamaljit   We're here to support our brothers. Their fight is our fight.

Tanvir   Very true, Kamaljit. This is a question of freedom, not religion. If we protect people's rights to be who they are, then they'll feel part of society. And there'll be more connection between all of us.

Kamaljit *regards* **Tanvir***, bowled over by his words.*

Kamaljit   It's all about . . . connection.

Reporter   Is this going to end with a man burning himself alive?

Tanvir   Not if the transport lot make the correct decision.

Reporter   So what should they do if a Turkish member of staff suddenly decides he wants to wear a fez?

Kamaljit   Why not? Live and let live, like the hippies say!

Reporter   Isn't this is a bit of a palaver for what is essentially a type of hat?

Tanvir   The turban is not a hat, it's a symbol of holiness, sacrifice, courage. In the last two world wars, thousands of Sikhs fought for this country with no other protection but their turbans. You take our turbans away, you take away our hearts. And a man is nothing without his heart.

Kamaljit   Well said, Tanvir.

Tanvir   Thank you, Kamaljit.

As the **Reporter** *retreats,* **Tanvir** *and* **Kamaljit** *look at each other, transfixed. The other protestors start a chant of 'Sikhs have rights' around them.*

Kamaljit's *chooni falls.* **Tanvir** *picks it up. Puts it back gently round her neck.*

Their eyes locked, **Tanvir** *and* **Kamaljit** *slowly join in the chanting as the protestors retreat.*

Scene Six

The shop. **Surinder** *reads her book whilst cleaning the counter. She tidies up and turns the sign on the door to CLOSED.*

Surinder (*reads to herself*)   Never in her life had she intended to do wrong; yet these hard judgements had come . . .

She closes the book. Starts to write with a pen.

Thomas Hardy indicates that life is not fair. But his decision to execute Tess after all that she has suffered, is an act of literary cruelty. Why not let his heroine live . . .

Suddenly **Jim** *bounds in, carrying a briefcase.*

Jim   Sorry I'm late . . . There's a right carry on going on out there. Massive crowd. TV cameras and everything.

Surinder   I should have locked the door. We're closed.

Jim   But I've got an appointment. With Mr Banga. Mr Tanvir Banga. About the chocolates. I'm Jim Wilson. What's your name?

Surinder   Surinder Bains.

Jim   Sue – rinder. How lovely. Sue Bains.

Jim *is entranced by her but covers and quickly composes himself.*

Do you like chocolate?

Surinder   Who doesn't?

Jim (*opening briefcase*)   You are in for a treat. I've been doing this job six months, and this is the best product I've had.

He takes out a box of chocolate bars.

It's all the rage in London. That's where I used to live. You ever been?

Surinder   No. Where do you live now?

Jim   Er, well . . . all over the place, a rep has to be nimble, travelling up and down. Means I've seen a bit of the world. Coventry, Gravesend, Swindon.

Surinder   Wow.

Jim   But London's the place. Full of artists, writers, musicians. They sit around in pubs and restaurants and discuss life, you know. How to make it kinder, softer . . .

He takes out the chocolate.

Surinder   Perhaps you should wait for Tanvir. I haven't got the money.

Jim   I can pop back another time. I'm always passing this way in the motor.

He holds a bar in front of her.

Surinder   I'd better not.

Jim   At least let me try out the patter. I need to practise.

She eyes the chocolate as though it's forbidden fruit.

Surinder   Alright.

A loud thudding sound from the back.

Jim   What was that?

Surinder   Probably my books falling off the kitchen table again. I always pile them too high.

Jim   You like books?

Surinder   Yeah.

Jim   So do I. They make my insides soar. Like a jumbo jet.

Surinder   Oh.

Jim   Shall I start?

Surinder *nods.* **Jim** *nervously clears his throat.*

Jim   Would you like to try the chocolate, Miss?

Surinder   Yeah.

Jim   Unwrap it. Let your eyes feast on the shiny foil and anticipate the adventure. Taste isn't the only sense that matters when it comes to flavour. Do you know what else . . .

Surinder (*interrupts*)   Smell.

Jim   That's what I was gonna say . . .

Surinder   As you chew, you're forcing air through your nasal passages, carrying the whiff of masticated food along with it. Without the interplay of taste and scent, humans wouldn't be able to grasp flavour. (*A beat.*) I'm doing biology O-level.

Jim   Right.

Surinder *sniffs the chocolate.*

Surinder   Smells a bit funny.

Jim   Funny can be new, different. Funny might be . . . sensational.

She eats a piece.

Surinder   It's got raisins in it.

Jim   Can you tell what the raisins taste of?

Surinder   Coke?

Jim *begins to sing* Jamaican Farewell.

Surinder   Tizer?

Jim *continues to sing.*

Beat.

Jim   Jamaican rum.

Surinder *spits it out, coughs and splutters.*

Surinder   I'm not allowed to drink.

Jim   You won't get drunk. Not from a couple of raisins.

Surinder   It's against my religion to drink.

Jim   I'm sorry, Sue. It's not real rum, only the flavour. They make it in the factory in Bromsgrove.

Surinder *composes herself. He stares at her, doesn't want to leave.*

Jim   You ever been to Catacombs?

Surinder   I sometimes walk through the graveyard on the way home from school.

Jim   It's a nightclub. In town.

Surinder   Not my kind of place.

Jim   What is your kind of place?

Surinder   Shop. Gurdwara. Laundrette.

Jim   There's a big world out there.

Surinder   Sounds like it.

Jim   In a speck of a second, the universe turns like a coin, from darkness to light and his being becomes whole . . .

Surinder   Eh?

Jim   Fact is, I'm a poet Sue. And I'm suddenly feeling . . . rather poetic. (*A beat.*) Because you're so sweet. Forgive me, I shouldn't have said that.

Embarrassed, he retreats to the door.

But you are Sue. You really are.

He heads out. **Surinder** *beholds the half-eaten chocolate bar and eats it, ravenously.*

She then picks up the radio, turns it on. The Monkees' Daydream Believer *plays.* **Surinder** *sings and dances as she cleans and organises the shop.*

Lost in her own world, she doesn't notice **Mrs Bains**, **Tanvir** *and* **Kamaljit** *enter. She continues swaying to the music.* **Mrs Bains** *turns the radio off.* **Surinder** *notices them, stops dead.*

Mrs Bains   Why didn't you lock the door?

Surinder   I thought I did.

Mrs Bains   Stupid!

Mrs Bains *locks the door.*

Kamaljit   You missed out, Surinder. Practically every single Sikh in England was there . . .

Tanvir   Felt like we were at Man United. All of us cheering at the Stretford End.

Kamaljit   And Tanvir's gonna be on the news.

Surinder   How come?

Tanvir   Reporter asked for my opinion.

Kamaljit   He was very eloquent. And . . . passionate.

Tanvir   No . . .

Kamaljit   You were . . . commanding.

Tanvir   Was I?

Mrs Bains   Has Daddy had his chah?

Surinder   I was just going to put the pan on.

Mrs Bains   I'll do it.

Mrs Bains *heads off.* **Kamaljit** *looks in the box, she beams.*

Kamaljit   Chocolate!

Surinder   The rep dropped it off.

Tanvir   I forgot about him!

Surinder   He dropped it off and left. Immediately. He was here for two minutes, actually only one minute . . .

Kamaljit   Suppose I'd better try one, then I can tell the customers how they taste.

Surinder   Don't! They're alcoholic.

Kamaljit   You've had one!

Surinder   I didn't realise.

Tanvir   She can have a piece!

Suddenly **Mrs Bains** *screams from the back.* **Tanvir** *rushes out.* **Kamaljit** *follows.*

Terror consumes **Surinder,** *she is frozen to the spot.*

After a few moments, **Kamaljit** *re-enters, she's in shock.*

Kamaljit   What were you doing?

Surinder   Nothing . . . I was here . . . what . . . what's happened?

Silence.

Surinder   Kamaljit?

Kamaljit   Did you check on Daddy?

No response.

Kamaljit (*loud*)   Did you check on him?

Surinder (*nods*)   I was about to get the pan. For his chah.

Kamaljit *slowly sits on the floor. She's in a daze.*

Surinder   Is he alright? He was alright a minute ago. Kamaljit, he was alright . . . He was.

She starts to cry as she drops to the floor, next to her sister.

On the other side of the stage, we see **Mrs Bains** *kissing and hugging her dead husband. Her body melts into his.*

Scene Seven

Bains' *living area. All the characters are onstage as if they are forming a congregation in a Gurdwara. They sit on the floor, their heads covered. They start singing a traditional Punjabi mourning song.*

Scene Eight

Hours later. **Mrs Bains** *quietly says a prayer as the characters move the furniture back. An empty space where* **Mr Bains** *used to sit.* **Surinder** *and* **Kamaljit** *tidy up.* **Tanvir** *sweeps the floor.* **Dhanda** *approaches the empty space.*

Dhanda   A man like him. A titan of a man. How can he be gone like this? (*A beat.*) He never fell before. Not once.

Tanvir   He never had a stroke before.

Dhanda   He must have heard the rallying call of the demonstration, yes . . . this Punjabi lion was trying to get to his people. (*A beat.*) At least there was no suffering. (*To* **Mrs Bains**.) Tell me again that he did not suffer.

Mrs Bains   The doctor said it would have been quick.

Dhanda   Lucky! Quick is the best way.

Kamaljit   How can there be a best way?

Dhanda   One day you will understand, Kamaljit beta [*dear*]. When you are old and broken. Your daddy's soul is free now. Blending with the divine, like a river rippling into the sea.

Kamaljit *starts to cry.* **Dhanda** *turns to her.*

Dhanda   Be strong beta. It is hard to bear. Yes. For me, especially. He was my father too. My father first. What that man lived. What that man saw in his years on this earth. The pain of Partition. You know he came from West Punjab, in a Muslim majority district. As a child he walked out of his house and saw his schoolmates hanging from neem trees. He dipped his hands into their wounds, wiping blood over his face so the attackers would leave him for dead. The family cut his hair short, Muslim style, and sent him alone on the back of a truck to escape to Delhi. My Birji would have joined us on the march that day. And he would be proud that our protest convinced the transport committee to change their minds. You know, I never wanted to buy a shop. It was he who encouraged me. Forced me. 'Go and make your mark, Patwant,' he said. He was mine and I was his. And now my soul is shattered into tiny pieces.

He holds back tears. **Kamaljit** *remains upset.*

Kamaljit   There can't be a God, Mum, there just can't.

Mrs Bains   No more crying! You think your daddy did crying? . . . My husband was a young man and this England made him old. He gave his life to this des [*country*] and it swallowed him, took him . . . from me . . . before he could become everything he was going to be . . . And he was close, so close . . .

Surinder *tentatively approaches her mother.*

Surinder   I'll be good now, Mum. For Daddy.

Mrs Bains   Your daddy is gone.

Surinder   I'll do anything you say.

Mrs Bains   There is nothing.

Kamaljit   The shop won't ever be the same.

Mrs Bains   The shop is the shop.

Dhanda   It is a pity he didn't see his daughters married.

Tanvir   Uncle, now is not the time to talk of weddings.

Dhanda   That time will come. Sooner than you think, Tanvir.

Mrs Bains   Kurreeyoh, go and change your clothes.

Surinder *and* **Kamaljit** *head out.*

Mrs Bains   Tanvir, check the shop front.

Tanvir   Why?

Mrs Bains   People should know we are open for business.

Tanvir   Today?

Mrs Bains   Today and every day.

He leaves. **Dhanda** *sits.*

Dhanda   Back home, it is tradition for a mourner to feed the bereaved family after the funeral. I should make your roti.

Mrs Bains   Our stomachs do not need to be full, at this moment.

They sit for a moment in silence.

Dhanda   You can be satisfied that you were a devoted wife. You have brought up two girls. Two good, simple girls.

Mrs Bains   I did my duty.

Dhanda   This shop is alive because of you, plus your bhindi [*okra*] is the tastiest in the whole of the West Midlands.

Mrs Bains   That is a matter of opinion.

Dhanda   If I had a wife like you, my life would be easier. Roti on the table every night, pressed shirt on the hanger, not too much talking at night-time.

Mrs Bains   Sarjit Bhanji will be back from India soon.

Dhanda   She is not coming back.

Mrs Bains   Why?

Dhanda   Sarjit is old. She does not feel like my wife any more.

Mrs Bains   Does she know this?

Dhanda   She is happy to stay in the pind. The cold weather and closed walls of Wolverhampton never suited her. There is something I want to suggest to you, Bhanji.

Mrs Bains   Er . . . I am very tired, Prahji, it has been a difficult day.

Dhanda   Of course. It is the start of many difficult days. A life with no man in the house is no life.

Mrs Bains   Tanvir is here.

Dhanda (*amused*)   Tanvir . . . Bhanji, there may be a way that I can alleviate some of your difficulties.

Mrs Bains   What way?

Dhanda   You have sweated blood in this country. You deserve peace. Relaxation. If you were to sell the shop, you could pay for the girls' weddings and still afford to retire respectably in India.

Mrs Bains   You want to buy the shop?

Dhanda   I am simply encouraging you to consider the future. A man works hard so that his mother, wife and daughters can be looked after. A shop is not something a woman can manage on her own.

Mrs Bains   Every single nook and cranny of this place is stained with my husband's toil and sweat. My girls and I will run it in his name, in his honour and we will make a better job of it than any man.

Dhanda   I understand. (*A beat.*) But how long will the girls be here to help? They can't be passing time with you and Tanvir forever.

Mrs Bains   No.

Dhanda   Have you started to look for boys?

Mrs Bains   We have just cremated your Birji.

Dhanda   Surinder is the one.

Mrs Bains   What do you mean?

Dhanda   That girl is your greatest asset.

Mrs Bains   She is my daughter.

Dhanda   Perhaps there will not be the need to search too far. If you are looking for a Jat, with a shop, someone with a British passport, of excellent character and someone who Birji would have approved of, your man may be closer than you think.

Mrs Bains   What . . . what do you mean?

Dhanda   The age gap between dearest Birji, God bless his soul, and yourself was not so different from the age gap between, say . . . Surinder and . . . me.

Mrs Bains   But . . . you have a wife.

Dhanda   Our marriage was never registered. So I am a free man.

Mrs Bains *takes this in.*

Dhanda   You know I would treat any wife of mine with the utmost kindness. My shop is thriving so you can be sure your daughter's future will be secure.

Mrs Bains   My daughter is young. Beautiful. She is still . . . like a child.

Silence.

Prahji, I am very tired. I need to rest now.

Dhanda   Of course, Bhanji. You give me your answer when you are ready.

He leaves. Shaken, **Mrs Bains** *watches him go.*

She stands alone, almost crumbles. Then gathers herself together.

Walks towards the telephone. Picks it up.

Scene Nine

Days later. The shop. **Mrs Bains** *and* **Surinder** *are stacking the shelves with goods.* **Tanvir** *brings in a cardboard box of Wagon Wheels.*

Tanvir   Who ordered Wagon Wheels?

Surinder   I didn't.

Tanvir   Stephen Burton and that lot keep asking for them. But Uncle said we shouldn't get any more because the rep tried to diddle him.

Mrs Bains   Those reps are all the same.

Surinder   Not all of them.

Tanvir   Should I put them out?

Mrs Bains   What?

Tanvir   It feels wrong. I mean . . . he didn't want them in the shop.

Mrs Bains   Stephen Burton wants them, stupid! Put them out and order more.

Tanvir *puts them out.* **Kamaljit** *enters.*

Kamaljit (*to* **Mrs Bains**)   Masi's [*Auntie*] on the phone. She says the pips are about to go.

Mrs Bains *hurries out.*

Surinder   Why isn't she phoning from the house?

Kamaljit   Maybe Masur's disconnected it again.

Tanvir   What's he do that for?

Kamaljit   He doesn't like her talking in case she tells people he has Bacardi and coke for breakfast.

Surinder   She only phones to make Mum cry. (*Mimics.*) Oh, your kismet is so bad. Two daughters, no son. And now your husband is dead and you are a widow. People will say you are a husband killer. And they will call me names because I am your sister. Hai hai my head hurts and I have a too weak bladder!

She feigns loud crying when suddenly **Jim** *stumbles into the shop.*

Kamaljit   Shop's not open.

Jim *flails around.*

Tanvir   We're doing a stock take!

Jim *moves towards him.*

Jim   You don't understand!

Tanvir *grabs a nearby mop and whacks* **Jim** *over the head with it.* **Jim** *falls to the floor.*

Surinder   Why did you do that?

Tanvir   I know his type. Hooligan!

Jim   I'm the chocolate fellah. Ask Sue . . .

Kamaljit   Sue?

Jim   I saw a gang of lads breaking into your van. I told them to get lost and one of them socked me in the face.

Tanvir *glances towards the window. He turns to* **Jim** *apologetically.*

Tanvir   Er . . . sorry about that, mate.

Jim   I don't reckon there's any damage but you might want to give it the once over.

Tanvir   Kamaljit, you should ask Mister . . .

Jim   Jim.

Tanvir   If he wants chah.

Kamaljit   But he's a gora.

Surinder   Kamaljit!

Kamaljit   What'll Mum say?

Surinder   Just go and make it!

Mop in hand, **Tanvir** *heads outside as* **Kamaljit** *goes to the kitchen.* **Jim** *contemplates* **Surinder**.

Jim   How have you been?

Surinder   The day you came . . .

Jim   Yeah?

Surinder   My dad died.

Jim   Sue, I'm so sorry . . .

Surinder   Happened when I was talking to you.

Jim   Oh, that's a lot . . . you poor thing . . .

Surinder   I keep thinking I'm getting used to it, but then I hear him shouting to put new labels in the price guns.

Jim   It's not your fault. People . . . die. We will all die. Cancer, road traffic accidents, some of us might even be murdered.

Surinder   Yeah.

Jim *begins to recite Dylan Thomas's poem,* Do Not Go Gentle Into That Dark Night.

Surinder   You like Dylan Thomas?

Jim   He's the master. I've sent him some of my work.

Surinder   Really?

Jim   He hasn't written back yet. (*A beat.*) I did walk by a couple of times but you must have been at school. Your brother was putting the bins out.

Surinder   Tanvir's not my brother. He's our helper, he lives in the cellar.

Jim   Thing is, Sue . . . you've become my inspiration.

Surinder   Me?

Jim   Since we met, words flow out of me. (*Clears his throat.*) My queen's hair is black. Her eyes as deep as a midnight lake . . .

Surinder   Carry on.

Jim   That's as far as I've got. I was wondering . . . if . . . I might be able to take you to the Golden Egg for a knickerbocker glory.

Surinder   I'm not allowed.

Jim   What?

Surinder   Out.

Jim   Where?

Surinder   Anywhere.

Jim   That's disappointing. I won't be in these parts much longer. I'm gonna try and make it big. London's calling me . . .

Like Dick Whittington . . . only, I'm gonna find the gold paved streets . . .

Tanvir *bustles in, triumphant.*

Tanvir   One look at my mop and they legged it.

Jim *can't tear his eyes away from* **Surinder**.

Tanvir   Got many uses, does a mop. Clean floor. Scare the mice away from the bread. Poke shoplifters. Play a tune when you're on your own behind the counter . . .

Tanvir *starts drumming a tune on the floor with the mop.*
Kamaljit *comes in with a tray of tea and biscuits.*

Jim *starts to go.*

Kamaljit   Wait, I've opened a packet of Orange Viscounts!

Jim   Better get to the motor in case those louts return. (*Low to* **Surinder**.) I'm usually down the Golden Egg on a Friday lunchtime for a gammon grill.

Bye, Sue.

Surinder   Bye.

He leaves. **Kamaljit** *fixes on the tea and biscuits.*

Surinder   Just eat them, Kamaljit!

Kamaljit *delves in.* **Surinder** *starts dancing to the mop beat.*

Kamaljit   How come he called you Sue?

Surinder   He brought the chocolates that day.

Kamaljit   You told him your name?

Surinder   He asked. And then he couldn't pronounce it.

Surinder   Don't tell Mum.

Kamaljit   What?

Surinder   I dunno . . . anything!

She grabs her sister and they dance together.

Kamaljit   I won't, I never would.

Surinder *breaks off and dances energetically.*

Kamaljit (*joking*)   You've got no sharam!

Surinder   Let's none of us have any sharam today, Kamaljit. Just for today!

She takes her sister and they dance into the next scene . . .

Scene Ten

Bains' *living area.* **Surinder** *sits in front of an open folder.* **Tanvir** *holds one of* **Surinder's** *text books.* **Kamaljit** *is on her haunches, kneading dough on the floor.*

Tanvir   What happened after the Wall Street Crash in 1929?

Mrs Bains *enters carrying clothes, she sits and starts to sew a kameez.*

Surinder   The loans given to Germany were recalled and the economy collapsed. Unemployment rocketed.

Tanvir   Affirmative.

Surinder *notices what* **Mrs Bains** *is doing.*

Surinder   That kameez doesn't fit me any more, Mum.

Mrs Bains   Why do you think I am taking apart the seam? This is good material, it shouldn't go to waste. (*A beat.*) You will need clothes.

Tanvir   And . . . what did the Enabling Act mean?

Surinder   That there was no political opposition to stop Hitler passing any laws.

Kamaljit (*to* **Surinder**)   You should be sewing your own kameez.

Tanvir   What year did Hindenberg die?

Kamaljit   I know this, 1936.

Surinder   Thirty-four.

Tanvir   Correct.

Kamaljit *gets up, having finished the dough.*

Mrs Bains   Kamaljit, choog [*check*] the dhal.

Kamaljit   I only just finished the atta. Why can't Surinder do it?

Surinder   I'm focusing on the Weimar Republic.

Kamaljit   Everything's easier for you.

Surinder   Tell Mum, not me.

Kamaljit   Mum!

Mrs Bains   Okay, Surinder, you go.

Surinder   Later.

Kamaljit   Now!

Surinder   I haven't got to Hitler yet.

Kamaljit   You just said he died!

Surinder   That was Hindenburg! If you'd stayed on at school you'd know the difference.

Kamaljit   I had to help in the shop and look after you.

Surinder   You didn't want to study, I like it.

Kamaljit (*low*)   More than you like hanging round the Golden Egg?

Surinder *throws her a concerned look.*

Mrs Bains   Surinder, fetch the dhal.

Surinder   This is my last paper, I need to finish World War Two by Friday.

Mrs Bains   You're going to your Masi's on Friday.

Kamaljit   Oh no . . .

Surinder   I can't afford to give up a weekend to go to Southall. They won't let me take history A-level if I don't pass this exam!

Mrs Bains (*interrupts*)   You're not doing any more stupid exams!

Surinder   What?

Mrs Bains   You're staying in Southall until Masi finds you a husband.

Shocked silence.

Mrs Bains   Both of you . . . Tanvir and I will manage the shop. After you are engaged, you will return here to get ready for your weddings. I've spoilt you. (*To* **Kamaljit**.) Letting you wither away behind the counter. (*To* **Surinder**.) Letting your mind go mad by reading books.

Surinder   You promised I could stay on.

Mrs Bains   There are men coming into this shop, looking at you in ways they should not be looking.

Surinder   That's not my fault.

Mrs Bains   I've decided.

Kamaljit   No . . .

Tanvir   Auntie, this is . . . this seems very fast. Perhaps take time to consider.

Mrs Bains   Nothing to consider. Your Masi and Masur will meet you at the train station on Friday.

Kamaljit   But . . . Mum . . .

Mrs Bains   But Mum what?

Kamaljit   What about what we want . . .

Mrs Bains   You, always you.

Kamaljit   You should have told us before, Mum.

Surinder   What's changed?

Mrs Bains   I've seen sense that's what. All this Tess and Tom and Hardy and Latin and biology and being so clever Miss Flan Flan nonsense. It's foolish thinking. Not for us. No. No, Sir . . . Daddy knew . . . when he was alive, he could look after you . . . I should have got you married back then

. . . because a married woman is a safe woman . . . Daddy knew . . . we are who we are and that's that.

Tanvir   Auntie . . .

Mrs Bains   And I don't need to hear any words from your big mouth. (*To* **Surinder**.) Go and get the tetchee cases from on top of the wardrobe.

Surinder *leaves.*

Kamaljit   Surinder, wait!

Kamaljit *and* **Tanvir** *appear frozen in shock.*

Agitated **Mrs Bains** *can't find something in her sewing box. She scuttles into the kitchen area.*

Tanvir *rushes up to* **Kamaljit**, *takes her hand.*

Tanvir   Kamaljit . . . I . . .

Kamaljit   Don't, Tanvir . . .

Tanvir   I can't let you . . .

Kamaljit *takes her hand away.*

Kamaljit   You have to forget . . .

Tanvir   Not while my feet are walking this earth. I'll find a way . . .

Mrs Bains *returns.*

Mrs Bains   Go through your clothes and pack the most simple suits. Don't choose nothing fancy.

Kamaljit *blankly heads off.*

Mrs Bains   Fill the stock for the morning.

Tanvir   Please, Auntie . . .

Mrs Bains   Fill the stock, Tanvir.

He leaves. **Mrs Bains** *puts the sewing down. Fights back tears.*

Scene Eleven

Bains' *living area. Two suitcases are on the stage.* **Kamaljit** *enters, wearing her coat. She contemplates the room.* **Surinder** *enters, picks up her coat, puts it on.*

Kamaljit   I don't want to go.

Surinder   You haven't got a choice.

Kamaljit   Aren't you bothered?

Surinder *takes an envelope out of her bag. Puts it on the side.*

Surinder   I can't say what I want . . . So I wrote Mum a letter. I put all my feelings in it. My real feelings, you know.

Tanvir *enters.*

Tanvir   Taxi's coming.

Kamaljit   I . . . don't feel well.

Tanvir   Would you like a glass of water, Kamaljit?

Kamaljit (*shakes head*)   Just need to sit for a minute.

He sits down next to her as **Mrs Bains** *bustles in.*

Mrs Bains   When they collect you, make sure you offer to pay for the petrol in your Masur's car. If they refuse the money, leave it on the mantelpiece. Always cover your head when your Masur is in the room. Remember, they are more traditional than us. You will not be able to flounce around like you do at home. Address everyone as Ji. If they ever have visitors, be sure to give up your bed and offer to sleep on the floor. Do not address your uncle unless he speaks first. Keep your head covered in his presence, do not laugh loudly, don't run anywhere and don't start eating until your Masur has finished.

Silence. **Mrs Bains** *starts to cry.*

Surinder   It's alright, Mum. We'll be alright.

Mrs Bains (*A beat*)   Go and wait for the taxi. And take your case.

Surinder *picks up her case, heads out.*

Mrs Bains   Tanvir, bring the other one. Kamaljit, check the shop is locked.

Kamaljit *goes.* **Tanvir** *picks up the other case, starts to head out and stops. He turns to* **Mrs Bains**.

Tanvir   I want to marry Kamaljit.

Mrs Bains   What did you say?

Tanvir   I want to marry Kamaljit.

Silence.

Tanvir   I know you think we are not well suited.

Mrs Bains   Of course you are not well suited.

Tanvir   I believe we are.

Mrs Bains   Hah, you are a stupid and she is a stupid.

Tanvir   Kamaljit and I have been reading the Granth Sahib and there are no words in there objecting to us getting married. I care for your daughter deeply. I respect you and Uncle, God rest his soul, too much to run away behind your back. And if you do not allow our union, I will obey your decision, leave the shop this very evening and spend the rest of my life alone and . . . celibate.

Mrs Bains   You are a lunatic.

Tanvir   If I am, so what? You know me, Auntie. I am honest and my hands are strong and I work all the hours God sends and if you allow it, I will treat Kamaljit like a precious diamond and I will be her servant until the day my heart stops beating.

Flustered, **Kamaljit** *hurries in.*

Mrs Bains   Wait with your sister.

Kamaljit   She's gone. Taken her case and everything.

She finds the note **Surinder** *left.*

Kamaljit   She . . . said she . . . wrote you a letter.

Mrs Bains   Read it. (*A beat.*) Read it!

Kamaljit (*opens letter*)   Dear Mum, I will not be going to Southall. I am not staying in Wolverhampton. Jim Wilson, the chocolate salesman has become a friend and is going to help me . . . I am sorry for the hurt this will cause. Please do not look for me, or try to contact me, and do not worry about me. I have taken my wedding jewellery. Your daughter, Surinder Kaur Bains.

Scene Twelve

Surinder *and* **Jim** *are in a London restaurant. They sit opposite one another at a table.* **Jim** *drinks a glass of red wine.*

Jim   I've paid for the bottle so don't be shy.

Surinder   Oh, I'm fine.

Surinder *ties up her hair.*

Jim   Such beautiful hair you've got . . . (*Clears throat.*) Her black mane gave him strength . . . She became his Samson . . . this brave lioness . . .

Surinder   Thank you. (*A beat.*) I've never cut my hair. It's against my religion.

Jim   Why?

Surinder   I can't say exactly . . .

Waitress brings two plates of steak and chips. Puts them in front of **Surinder** *and* **Jim**.

Jim   Is this your first meal in a restaurant?

Surinder *nods.*

Surinder   What is it?

Jim   Steak.

Surinder   Beef?

Jim   Yeah.

Surinder   I haven't eaten beef before.

Jim   This is going to be a fine moment then.

Surinder   I'm not even that hungry.

Jim   I've ordered it now.

Surinder *nervously picks up her knife and fork, cuts off a bit of the steak, puts it in her mouth.* **Jim** *pours her some red wine, hands it to her.*

Jim   Wash it down with this.

She drinks it. Sits back. Breathes hard.

Jim   He found the damsel, scooped her up from the inferno, placed her in paradise. (*A beat. Indicates steak.*) What do you think?

Surinder   It's a . . . foreign flavour . . .

Jim   Because it's Français. (*A beat.*) Means a lot to me, you know. That you believe so deeply.

Surinder   What?

Jim   In my writing.

Surinder   Oh.

Jim   Now my muse is by my side, I shall write every day. And with a decent body of work, I'll have a better chance of being published. You've made your dream happen, Sue, and it's given me hope that I can do the same.

Surinder   My dream?

Jim   Coming to London. With me.

Surinder   You know . . . I . . . er . . . had a kind teacher at school, she taught me about books . . . made me love learning.

Jim   How nice.

Surinder   I think my true dream would be to pass that love on. Become a teacher like her.

Jim   For now, I've got you a job in a wireless factory and you'll be looking after the bedsit. Once I'm on the ascent, it'll be your turn to fly.

Surinder   When might that be?

Jim   Give me a chance. When you get home from work, you can read my poems, help me decide which are the best ones to send.

Surinder   Actually, Jim, I . . . really do want to study.

Jim   Right.

Surinder   I could sell some of my jewellery, use it to pay for a college course.

Jim   Your jewellery?

Surinder *nods.*

Jim   I've already sold it.

Surinder   What?

Jim   I had to put a deposit down on the bedsit. I couldn't have you living in some dive. I want you to be comfortable.

Surinder   All of it? You sold all my gold?

Jim (*nods*)   Everything's about us now, Sue. You and me finding light in this dark world. Plus, this city's not cheap. One of us has to be responsible.

Shocked **Surinder** *plays with her food.*

Jim   Don't you want your steak?

Surinder It just tastes so . . . strange.

*An echo of the movement section which showed **Mr Bains**'s decline. This time, **Mrs Bains** ends up lying on the makeshift bed.*

Scene Thirteen

*Years later. The **Bains**' living area has been spruced up. **Dhanda** and **Tanvir** sit, drinking tea. **Tanvir** now wears glasses. Both men and **Kamaljit** have aged well. An infirm **Mrs Bains** lies in the space previously occupied by her husband.*

*On another part of the stage, dishevelled, **Jim** sits on a bed in a bare bedsit space. **Surinder** is cleaning the floor. She appears world weary, older than her still tender years.*

Dhanda Did I mention I am buying next door?

Mrs Bains Shut up, stupid, fucking bastard, kutha, haramjada!

Tanvir Curly the greengrocers?

Dhanda The man is an alcoholic who is making a loss. I'm giving him a fair price and he is moving to the Costa del Sol. I will extend the stock room and sell garam masala, green chillis and coriander.

Tanvir Who will buy those? People want hamburger, pizza, fish fingers.

Dhanda We shall see.

*He takes out some sheets of paper. **Tanvir** reads.*

Dhanda Sign and I'll be on my way. Seeto is cooking lamb kofte and jalebi. She starts to sulk if I eat her food cold. Plus little Ranjit misses his daddy if I am gone too long.

Tanvir (*reads*) You want our children to be learning Punjabi and Sikhi in schools?

Dhanda Their mother tongue. And their religion.

Kamaljit (*offstage*)   It's here!

Kamaljit *wheels in a trolley containing the entire Encyclopaedia Britannica.*

Dhanda   What is this?

Kamaljit   Encyclopaedia Britannica. He's been saving up for ages.

Jim *starts to pace around.*

Tanvir *takes a tome and starts flicking through.*

Jim   I don't have no luck. Not ever.

Surinder   Maybe look for a sales job again.

Jim   That's not me any more. Not me, at all. (*A beat.*) I need to lend some money.

Surinder   You mean borrow. You need to borrow some money.

Jim   We could sell something.

Surinder   There's nothing. (*A beat.*) The landlord asked if I might be able to help with his accounts.

Jim   What?

Surinder   I've said yes.

Jim   He asked because he fancies you.

Surinder   No. Because I can read and write and because I've got half a brain.

Stressed **Jim** *goes to look for something.*

Tanvir *indicates the encyclopaedia to* **Dhanda**.

Tanvir   Kamaljit and I will read a few pages each day. Knowledge will free us.

Dhanda   In this country, money is the path to freedom. They tore us down. Now we have risen and we run things.

He indicates the papers.

Sign, please. We must make sure our children learn to behave nicely, according to our rules.

Tanvir   Uncle . . . Sikhi, true Sikhi comes from love, not control. You want us to live in a little Punjab when we are in Wolverhampton.

Dhanda   Punjab is a state of mind Tanvir. Nobody owns land. On this earth, a person has a right to move from one location to another. We maintain our identity so we can be ourselves.

Tanvir   We can be us here. With the goreh.

Dhanda   Then we will be inviting chaos.

Tanvir   You sound like Enoch.

Dhanda   No . . .

Tanvir   Filled with foreboding; like the Roman, I see the River Tiber foaming with much blood.

Dhanda   Kamaljit's father, my dear Birji, would have signed without reading a single word, because he trusted me. We lived something. We lived something. Together. You remember how the goreh used to look at us, how they shamed us. If we start to mix up with them, then who do we become? Because they take from you Tanvir, they take and they take and they take! (*Gets up.*) When you are ready to sign, let me know.

Tanvir (*A beat*)   I will not be signing, Uncle. Not this or any other petition you bring.

Awkward silence. **Dhanda** *starts to exit.*

Dhanda   My ears are ringing, little Ranjit must be crying for me. I pray one day you experience the love only a son can give.

Kamaljit   We both pray.

Dhanda   Did I mention I am extending the shop?

Tanvir   You did.

Dhanda   It will be double the size. I want my boy to witness his father's ambition. (*A beat.*) You should consider updating your stock, Tanvir. Shop front is looking too old-fashioned. (*To* **Mrs Bains**.) Sat Siri Akal, Bhanji.

Mrs Bains   Shut up stupid, fucking bastard, kutha, haramjada!

He leaves. **Tanvir** *continues to read.*

Jim *is getting increasingly frustrated.*

Jim   Where's my book? I shall compose a brand new poem. And then maybe a short story . . . yes, that's it. Fiction will be my new path . . .

Surinder   Will you please stop!

Jim   What?

Surinder   Has a single sentence, no . . . has a single word ever made you a penny?

Jim   Not yet . . . but . . .

Surinder   Not yet, not ever. Never. Ever. Can't you see . . .

Jim   This is typical of you.

Surinder   We don't have any money!

Jim   You look so beautiful. If only you could act how you look.

Surinder   I can't do this any more . . . Jim . . . .

Jim   You really don't love me. You actually don't . . .

Surinder   I left my family for you. I let myself become a story that gets passed round people's lips . . .

Jim   You left because you didn't want to marry some stranger. (*A beat.*) You don't care. And now, you won't even deny it.

Kamaljit *faces* **Tanvir**.

Kamaljit   Uncle does care about us.

Tanvir   He cares about driving a Mercedes Benz.

Kamaljit   I would like my child to grow up knowing the history of the Gurus and to read the Granth Sahib. And to love their culture.

Tanvir   I would like my child to go to the finest schools, to cheer for England in the World Cup and eat Yorkshire pudding on a Sunday.

Kamaljit   Maybe our child can do both.

Tanvir *picks up another volume.*

Kamaljit   Tanvir!

She takes his hand, places it on her tummy.

Kamaljit   I said, maybe our child can do both.

Overjoyed, he picks her up, spins her around.

Tanvir   This is the best day. The very best day.

Slowly, **Kamaljit** *turns to her mum.*

Kamaljit   A new beginning's coming, Mum.

Mrs Bains *stares at her.*

Kamaljit   Everything that's passed . . . we won't have to think about it any more.

Surinder   I wish I could cut pieces of my body off and send them back home.

Jim   What are you saying?

Surinder   At least then I'd be there. (*A beat.*) I miss my mum slapping me round the face. So much. Do you miss your mum?

Jim   Stop talking nonsense . . . I love you so much. I love you and it barely registers . . .

Surinder   You love a story, Jim. That's not me. It was never me.

Jim   You're supposed to be my rock, my Samson . . .

Suddenly **Surinder** *gets up, frantically starts looking for something.*

Jim   What are you doing?

She finds some scissors, faces **Jim**. *We don't know what she's going to do. She starts cutting her hair.*

Jim   Stop . . . stop . . . please . . .

Surinder   One of us has to walk into the real world. Make money.

Jim   Not your hair . . .

Surinder   It's mine, Jim. It's the one thing that's still . . .

Clumps of her black tresses fall to the floor.

Jim   Who's going to want that now?

Surinder   Somebody will, Jim. (*A beat.*) Somebody.

Interval.

Act Two

Scene One

Present day. The **Bains**' *living area retains a couple of bits of furniture/photos from the years before. But it has been brought up to date in a blank DFS way. Condolence cards are dotted around.* **Ranjit** *sits, manspreading enthusiastically whilst checking his phone. There's a carrier bag on the floor.* **Arjan** *brings in two mugs of tea, hands one to* **Ranjit***.*

They drink their tea. **Ranjit** *eyes the contents of* **Arjan**'s *mug.*

Ranjit   What the hell's that?

Arjan   Camomile.

Ranjit   Stick some milk in it, you pindoo [*villager*].

Arjan   It's herbal.

Ranjit *takes this in.*

Ranjit   Have you gone gay?

Arjan   Yeah.

He looms over **Ranjit** *and pretends to try to kiss him. They tussle.*

Ranjit   Get off! (*A beat.*) Anyway, I like gays.

Arjan   Eh?

Ranjit   They're all down the gym, aren't they? One of them's gonna buy my Peloton.

Arjan   You said the touchscreen broke.

Ranjit   He only wants it for Pilates and shit.

He indicates **Arjan**'s *tea.*

Ranjit   Don't you drink chah no more?

Arjan   Camomile's soothing.

Ranjit   If you want soothing, I'll sort you out. I'm buying you a lap dance later.

Arjan   No thanks.

Ranjit   We'll go up the Red Lion then. Have a few glassies.

Arjan   I'm looking after my mum.

Ranjit   What do you think the old ladies are for? (*A beat.*) Come on, I've missed you, chitterface [*bumface*].

Arjan   Another time, Ranjit.

Ranjit   Nobody calls me that anymore. It's Jay, yeah?

Ranjit *indicates the carrier bag.*

Ranjit   Show us then.

Arjan *takes it out. Holds up a smart blue suit.*

Arjan   He liked blue. He looked good in blue.

Ranjit *feels the material.*

Ranjit   Oh yeah. This is quality, man. Quality. Will he be wearing this when they stick him in the furnace?

Arjan   Yes.

Ranjit   Shame he won't get to wear it again. (*A beat.*) How much was it?

Arjan   Three.

Ranjit   Quid?

Arjan   Hundred!

Ranjit   Are you mad? I could have got you this shit for forty, fifty pound.

Arjan   I can afford it, Ranjit.

Ranjit   Jay! (*A beat.*) You still doing that gora job?

Arjan   I'm a creative director. You know I'm a creative director.

Ranjit   Didn't you study painting and decorating?

Arjan   Fine art.

Ranjit   I know, I'm only messing. You wanna get a property.

Arjan   I've got a property.

Ranjit   Use the equity to get another one. And then another one. Then you can be like me.

Arjan   I enjoy my job.

Ranjit   Is your goree coming?

Arjan   Her name's Claire.

Ranjit   I like her. She looks . . . clean. Tell her to cover her legs and sit with the women.

Arjan   She knows.

Kamaljit *and* **Dhanda** *enter. Both have aged.* **Ranjit** *springs up.*

Ranjit   Sat siri akal, Auntie.

Kamaljit   Sat siri akal, beta.

She busies herself tidying.

Ranjit   Sit down.

Kamaljit   I'm better standing up.

Ranjit   Dad.

Ranjit *offers his seat to* **Dhanda** *who sits. He gets emotional.*

Dhanda (*to* **Arjan**)   Your daddy was like my own skin and bones. My first son. When he and your mummy were married, in the absence of his father, I did the Milni. You remember, Kamaljit?

Kamaljit   Yes, Uncle.

Dhanda　We exchanged blankets. Big fat woollen ones. (*To* **Kamaljit**.) Do you still have those blankets?

Kamaljit　Er . . . somewhere.

Dhanda　Tanvir was a better man than other men. He had a big heart. So his heart attack must also have been very big.

Arjan *shows his mum the suit.*

Arjan　What do you think?

Kamaljit　It's blue.

Arjan　Yes.

Kamaljit　Blue reminds me of toilet cleaner.

Ranjit　I know what you mean, Auntie.

Arjan　I can change it, if you like.

Kamaljit　Don't be stupid. Your dad won't mind.

Ranjit　Course he won't.

Dhanda　I was his elder. I should have gone first.

Ranjit　Stop that talk, Dad.

Dhanda　You don't worry, Kamaljit. I will be by Arjan's side. Show him the ropes.

Kamaljit　Thank you, Uncle.

Dhanda (*to* **Arjan**)　This thing we are about to do is no easy thing. When you next see your daddy, you will smell a smell you have never smelt before. And you will see his face and it will be another face. You know a dead man's lips are purple. Like a child who has spent all the day sucking an ice lolly. There will be the usual fluids that ooze from a live body.

Ranjit　Like when a baby's born. That ain't no Yummy Mummies on Insta. Shit and piss all the way, brother.

Dhanda　Once we have washed the body, he will be a king, ready to return to his kingdom. You don't be scared, Arjan.

Arjan　I'll manage.

Dhanda   Would Tanvir like one of his Encyclopaedia in the coffin?

Kamaljit   I don't think he'll be able to read it.

Dhanda   I will instruct the Gurdwara Committee to alert their top Giani for the funeral.

Arjan   I've already called them, Uncle. Thanks for your guidance with the washing, but everything else, well it's up to me now . . .

Ranjit   Dad's trying to help, brother.

Dhanda   It's okay, Arjan, it's okay . . .

He puts a kind arm around **Arjan**.

Dhanda   Ranjit will drive us.

Arjan   I'll meet you there.

Dhanda *goes.* **Ranjit** *follows.* **Kamaljit** *picks up the cups.*

Kamaljit   Uncle's missing your daddy. Try and talk nicely to him.

Arjan   He's here every single day. And Ranjit.

Kamaljit   You two used to play Lego.

Arjan   When I was five. Ranjit's . . . an actual moron.

Kamaljit   And you're not an actual moron? Uncle looked after us when my daddy died and after Mum . . . He did things for us that you can't understand. People aren't the way you'd like them to be, that's how it is.

Arjan (*A beat*)   I'm not sure Dad would have wanted this.

Kamaljit   What?

Arjan   Washing his body. The prayers. Planning to take his ashes to a village he never visited. He might have preferred it if we scattered him on the pavement outside the shop, then he could stay close to us.

Kamaljit   It's not about what he wanted.

Arjan   What is it then?

Kamaljit   Your dad doesn't have to go to the Gurdwara any more. I do.

Arjan   You don't have to go.

Kamaljit   What else am I supposed to do? When I walk in and the ladies' eyes pierce me with their pity, I plan to hold my head up high. Say I did all the proper, traditional things for my husband. Then, and only then, can I start chopping onions with the rest of them.

She picks up a glasses case. Takes out **Tanvir**'s *glasses, beholds them.*

Arjan   Shall we put those on him?

Kamaljit *puts the glasses on.*

Arjan   Mum, what are you doing?

Kamaljit   Keeping him close.

Arjan   You'll mess your eyes up!

She starts walking around but she can barely see.

Kamaljit   I don't care.

She wanders aimlessly and bumps into a chair.

He said when we got old we'd go to the cinema every Tuesday.

Arjan   That's nice.

Kamaljit   Twenty per cent off on a Tuesday.

Arjan   I remember when I was little, he'd bring a family pack of popcorn from the shop and empty it out into three cartons.

Kamaljit (*fondly*)   He was so cheap.

Arjan   You and me, we could go to the cinema.

Kamaljit   I don't want to go to the cinema with you.

Arjan   If you like you can come and stay with me in London.

Kamaljit   London smells of wee.

Arjan   Move outside Wolverhampton then. Buy a cottage in the countryside.

Kamaljit   Why?

Arjan   More space, you can potter around in the garden.

Kamaljit   What's the point of that?

Arjan   Just an idea.

Kamaljit   Who'll run the shop?

Arjan   You can't keep the shop, Mum, not without Dad.

Kamaljit   Your father might be gone but he's still my husband. And this . . . here . . . is what we do. What we've always done.

Arjan   You can't even drive. How will you get to the cash and carry?

Kamaljit   There are buses . . .

Arjan   What can I do?

Kamaljit   Have I ever asked you for anything?

Arjan   No.

Kamaljit   You have your flat. Your office. That girl.

Arjan   I need to know you're gonna be okay.

Kamaljit   Let me do what I want, and you do what you want.

Arjan (*A beat*)   I want Dad not to be gone.

Kamaljit *takes off the glasses.*

Kamaljit   You always had your head high up in the clouds
. . .

She puts the glasses on **Arjan**.

Kamaljit   . . . just like him.

Scene Two

Bains' *living area.* **Arjan** *is with* **Claire**. *She signals towards the kitchen.*

Claire   I should give your mum a hand.

Arjan   I wouldn't . . .

Claire   I found a YouTube video about how to make rotis.

Arjan   It's fine . . .

Claire   Isn't the daughter-in-law supposed to make rotis?

Arjan   Not necessarily . . . Mum can be quite . . . particular in the kitchen.

Claire   Particular?

Arjan   My dad watched a show about Mussolini once and decided to make a lasagne. He used the wrong pan for the meat and put atta . . . chappati flour in the white sauce . . . when Mum saw the state of the worktop . . . she threatened to kill him and screamed so loud that a customer called the police.

Claire   I'll leave her to it.

They share a warm laugh.

Arjan   I mean obviously she didn't . . . kill him, because he's just died.

Arjan*'s about to break,* **Claire** *holds him.*

Arjan   The whole world feels different, Claire.

Claire   Bound to. He's not in it any more.

She takes his hand, strokes it tenderly.

What you said at the crematorium was . . . perfect and true.

Arjan   I meant it. All of it.

Claire   I learned a lot from him reading the encyclopaedias out loud. The confidence when he recited the periodic table that time . . .

Arjan   Knew all the halogens . . .

Claire   And the noble gases.

Arjan   He said once you understand something, deeply understand it, your mind's free to learn the next thing and the next. You know, if he'd had an education, my dad would have done some stuff. Big stuff . . .

Claire   Your dad did plenty. (*A beat.*) I don't think it's really hit your mum.

Arjan (*A beat*)   She wants to keep the shop.

Claire   Thought you said she'd be selling.

Arjan   Not yet. I'm going to help her out for a bit, you know.

Claire   No question.

Arjan   Yeah.

Claire   When are work expecting you back?

Arjan   They said when I'm ready.

Claire   Good.

Arjan   This won't affect the wedding.

Claire   I'm not thinking about the wedding. (*A beat.*) Arj, I'm here for you. Even when I'm not here.

They kiss. **Bill** *enters.*

Bill   Toilet won't flush.

Claire (*embarrassed*)   Dad.

Bill   I tried everything. Brute force, quick-fire motion, a deft flick of the wrist. But . . . nothing.

Arjan   Don't worry. I'll sort it.

Bill   Where's Cameljeet?

Claire   Kitchen.

Bill   Excellent. (*A beat.*) You don't think she'll want to relieve herself soon, do you? Just because . . . er . . . I don't want her to go in there and er . . . I'd rather not cause any distress . . . not on a day like today . . . do you know what I mean?

Arjan   It's fine, Bill.

Bill   I hope she hasn't gone to too much trouble.

Arjan   It's no trouble.

Silence.

Bill   Would you mind sorting the flush out? Only it's going to play on my mind.

Arjan *heads out.* **Bill** *and* **Claire** *stand in silence.*

Bill   I couldn't help . . .

Claire   Don't, just don't . . .

Bill   There's obviously a plumbing issue . . .

Claire   Will you stop going on about it?

Bill   Is it beef they don't eat?

Claire   Yes.

Bill   But pork's alright? Bacon, ham, sweet and sour . . .

Claire   Yes!

Bill   I'm only checking. I don't want to say the wrong thing.

Claire   Then please stop talking.

Arjan *comes back.*

Arjan   Sorted.

Bill   Thank God.

Awkward silence.

Such a nice man, your dad.

Arjan   He was.

Bill   I wish I'd got to know him better. Do you have any other family round here?

Arjan   No, my mum had a sister but she died.

Bill   Oh dear and now your mum has to cope with this.

Arjan   Her sister died a long time ago, when she was sixteen. Car crash.

Bill   Was she wearing a seatbelt?

Arjan   Er . . . I'm not aware . . .

Claire   He wasn't alive, Dad.

Bill   My old optician used to say that before the seatbelt law came in, people's faces used to regularly smash through the windscreen. Into smithereens! The doctors in A and E spent most Saturday evenings stitching noses and lips back together. Once the law was passed, the bodies stopped piling in. Practically overnight, he said. That's good, isn't it?

Silence.

Is it beef you Sikhs don't eat?

Arjan   It's more of a cultural choice.

Bill   But why beef?

Arjan   I don't actually know.

Claire   It doesn't matter.

Kamaljit *comes in, she holds a cloth and cleans around the place.*

Kamaljit   Food is almost ready.

Bill   Can you enlighten me, Cameljeet? As to why Sikhs don't eat beef.

Kamaljit   We don't eat beef.

Bill   Why though?

Kamaljit   We just don't.

Bill   Got it.

Claire *gets up to offer* **Kamaljit** *her chair.*

Kamaljit   It's okay.

Claire   Please.

Kamaljit *continues cleaning.*

Arjan   Sit down for a minute, Mum!

Kamaljit *stops. She cleans the seat where* **Claire** *has been sitting and sits down.*

Claire   Arjan says you're holding onto the shop.

Bill   Are you?

Kamaljit   Yes.

Claire   I suppose you'd miss the customers.

Kamaljit   I don't like the customers. And they don't like me.

Arjan   That's not true, Mum.

Kamaljit   They always asked for him.

Arjan   Amy Burton likes you.

Kamaljit   You know she has eleven children. And they say us Asians have big families. The latest boyfriend is a tattoo artist. He practises on the kids. No shortage of space there.

Bill   Everyone's always stuffing their faces these days.

Kamaljit   They are.

Bill   And it's on the telly all the time, isn't it? Food.

Arjan   The programmes are cheap to make.

Bill   But they're in Tuscany or Sri Lanka every week! I couldn't afford Tuscany or Sri Lanka.

Claire   It's still relatively cheap.

Bill   You've got no idea about money.

Claire   I did maths A-level.

Bill   You don't even know if you're getting married in a few months. I mean, what if you lose your deposit for the venue?

Claire   I don't care about the deposit.

Bill   See, you can't manage your own life.

Claire   I can and I do!

Awkward silence. **Kamaljit** *gets up to go.*

Kamaljit   Better check the sabji.

Arjan   Bill, why don't you help Mum with the plates?

Bill   Certainly.

Bill *follows* **Kamaljit** *out.*

Claire   He's so fucking embarrassing.

Arjan   Forget it.

Claire   It's like he's got . . . no love in him.

Arjan   Don't say that.

Claire   Him and my mum . . . it wasn't like with your parents.

Arjan   He must have some love. He made you.

Claire   Did your mum really meet your dad when she was fifteen?

Arjan (*nods*)   They both said it was love at first sight. And after all these years, my dad told me he still felt like the luckiest man in Wolverhampton.

Claire (*A beat*)   She's going to be lonely, isn't she? When you come back to London.

Arjan   Yeah.

Claire   If she wants to move in with us after the wedding, I'm completely open to living as part of a multi-generational, extended family . . .

Arjan   She doesn't want to move in.

Claire   We could look into supported accommodation. So she's got company.

Arjan   Company?

Claire   And so she's safe.

Arjan   You mean like an old people's home?

Claire   I didn't say that . . .

Arjan   My mum is not old.

Claire   I'm talking about . . . housing, with somebody nearby, like a warden . . .

Arjan   This place is all she's ever known.

Claire   You're misinterpreting my words . . .

Arjan   Claire, I'm staying here. And I don't know how long for, okay.

Claire   Of course.

Arjan   While she needs me, I'm staying.

Scene Three

The shop. **Arjan** *is organising shelves in the shop. A drunk white guy,* **Tommy,** *enters. Flails around.*

Tommy Alright, Arj . . .

Arjan Tommy.

Tommy Where's Tanvir?

Arjan He's dead, remember.

Tommy Oh . . . yeah . . . fuck . . . yeah . . . I miss the bones of that man. Your dad . . . he was a fucking giant . . . I loved that geezer . . . I would have even gone to his funeral if I had the right date . . . bet you did all the rituals and singing and that, didn't you?

Arjan Yeah.

Tommy I knew it! You lot are kings of that shit . . . that culture shit . . . We've lost it . . . lost our souls . . . our people don't know what to do when pain strikes . . . fuck . . . I loved that man . . . like he was my dad . . .

Arjan Sure . . .

Tommy Me and him used to discuss things, you know . . . important things. Life things. I miss those days . . .

Arjan Yeah.

Tommy I was telling him, Arj . . . the AI's coming for us. It's gonna like . . . be injected into the bloodstream . . . and next they're gonna put chips in our brains . . . and . . . my brother already lost his job at the Council . . . you know he had a decent job . . . in a office . . . and they got rid of him . . . you know . . . just like that . . . and now he's staring at his phone, day and night . . . he sits there.

Arjan That's a shame, mate.

Tommy Your dad used to say people are always moving. You can't stop them moving . . . exploring new lands . . . but

I told him . . . there aren't enough . . . doctors' surgeries or schools or KFCs, do you know what I mean? He said it was down to resources and the government hasn't invested and all that and . . . I mean why can't people just stay put . . . in France or some other shithole . . . They're letting the whole world onto our shores. The whole fucking world . . . and my brother hasn't even got his job any more . . .

He picks up a load of goods, almost falls over as he puts them on the counter.

Arjan   I can't serve you, Tommy.

Tommy   Why?

Arjan   You owe us almost fifty quid.

Tommy   Your dad won't mind. He knows I always pay up . . .

Arjan   And you've had too much to drink.

Tommy   Don't go social services on me, Arj . . . come on . . .

Arjan   No.

Tommy   Your dad would have served me . . .

Arjan   No he wouldn't. Go home.

Tommy   Home?

Arjan   Yeah.

Tommy   You've made a mistake there . . .

Arjan   How's that?

Tommy   Because this is my home. Everywhere you see is my house. Not yours.

Arjan   Get out . . .

Tommy   You think because you've got all these fags and tins of beans and packets of sugar . . . that you're better than me . . . who was on the land this shop's built on, first?

Arjan   I said leave!

Tommy   Plus . . . I don't have you lot as mates! Not shit-stained Pakis from Pakistani land.

Arjan   Fuck off.

Tommy   You are in my country! My white country.

Tommy *squares up to* **Arjan** *who aggressively stares into his face. Suddenly* **Tommy** *does a Nazi salute.*

Arjan (*shouts*)   Get the fuck out.

Tommy *staggers and crashes into a stack of tins. They roll onto the floor.* **Tommy** *stumbles and takes a swing at* **Arjan** *who deftly catches him and harshly chucks him out.*

Arjan *eyes the mess. Kicks the tins in fury.*

Scene Four

Ranjit's *shed. Assorted junk.* **Ranjit** *devours a chicken leg from a box. Offers the box to* **Arjan** *who shakes his head.*

Arjan   I'm not hungry.

Ranjit   Man needs bare protein if he wanna get hench.

Arjan   I don't wanna get hench.

Ranjit   What if that piece of shit comes back and fucks with you?

Arjan   I could have had him, easy.

Ranjit   But you didn't, did you? He got away.

Arjan   He was drunk. I think he's got mental health issues.

Ranjit   You ain't in London now, brother. We have to take care of ourselves in these endz. What you gonna do next time your drunk mentally ill friend passes round? With his mates? What if your mum's behind the counter on her own? You gonna show him how to do reiki or mindfulness or some shit?

Ranjit *finds a huge suitcase. Opens it.*

Ranjit   Take a look at these babies, chitterface [*bumface*].

Arjan   What the fuck?

Ranjit   Pretty, aren't they?

Arjan   Is this . . . even legal?

Ranjit   Man don't business with the feds.

Arjan *takes out an assortment of weapons.*

Ranjit   Those are an exact replica of the nunchucks Bruce Lee had in Enter the Dragon. And that is a katana. Careful brother, this shit could cut your hand off.

Arjan   What the hell are you doing with all this?

Ranjit   When you're a kid helping in the shop and you watch your dad being shat on day in day out, you make yourself a man. And man needs protection. Do you fancy a samurai sword?

Arjan   No!

Ranjit   Take something, you bhenjot [*sisterfucker*]!

Arjan *eyes a stick, balanced against a wall.*

Arjan   What's that?

Ranjit   My mum's mop.

Arjan *picks it up.* **Ranjit** *starts to build a spliff.*

Ranjit   It's good you're home, brother. Back where you belong. What do you do in London anyway?

Arjan   Work. See friends.

Ranjit   You can do that in Wolverhampton. How big's your house down there?

Arjan   It's a flat.

Ranjit   You seen my house, innit?

Arjan   Yeah.

Ranjit   Five bedrooms. Me and my missus have our own dressing rooms. You know how many buy-to-lets I've got now?

Arjan   Four?

Ranjit   Nineteen.

He lights the spliff. Takes a long drag. Hands it to **Arjan**.

Ranjit   Shop's hard graft, innit?

Arjan   Yeah. I mean . . . it's just me and Mum.

Ranjit   Pressure, brother.

Arjan   Yeah.

Ranjit   Pure pressure. On your head and your heart . . . the females of the species don't understand what us lot have to bear.

Arjan   I just wanna be able to walk up the road feeling free, you know . . . just walk up the road and breathe.

Ranjit (*A beat*)   I get you, brother. Me and Dad are here for you. We're family. You know that?

Arjan   Appreciate it. (*A beat.*) You've got masis and bhuas and chachas and cousins . . . blood and biology everywhere you look. You're lucky.

Ranjit   I don't fuckin' know . . .

Arjan   You are.

Ranjit   When you're a son in the middle of the bed, you get spoilt with Xbox and PlayStation and shit. And one day there's half a million in your account, but everything costs, brother.

Arjan   How?

Ranjit You're the future, the hope of the whole Khandan. They gotta believe you're gonna take care of all the shit. Cos if you fuck it up, then the bad looks and the chat from out there's gonna land. And suddenly the whole family goes down. And it's on you. (*A beat.*) You got away, Arj.

Arjan Now I'm back, I wanna do the right thing, you know.

Ranjit The right thing, brother. That's why I keep my chin up. Face out front. New buy to let and motor every two years. When they see that, they can have faith. (*A beat.*) You don't have this shit in London.

Arjan There's different shit.

Ranjit Maybe I'll come and visit one day.

Arjan Yeah.

Ranjit You'll have to take me on the Eye and up the Shard and all that. (*A beat.*) Will you take me?

Arjan Sure. (*A beat.*) You ever thought about making a different choice?

Ranjit (*A beat*) What would I wanna do that for?

He gets up, picks up a weapon and brandishes it around.

Ranjit Gotta keep myself fit and strong, brother. So I can show up for the likes of you. (*A beat.*) I mean it's not like you can ask your Masi to help out.

Arjan What?

Ranjit Your mum's sister.

Arjan Of course not, she died, Ranjit.

Ranjit My dad was talking about her the other night.

Arjan Did he tell you she was killed in a car crash?

Ranjit Probably been better if she had.

Arjan What do you mean?

Ranjit   He said she ran off with a gora.

Arjan   Eh?

Ranjit *takes the spliff back.*

Ranjit   Big scandal, brother.

Arjan   Are you saying . . . my Surinder Masi . . . is alive?

Ranjit   Yeah.

Arjan   Where is she?

Ranjit   Dunno.

Arjan   Are you being fucking serious?

Ranjit   Why would I lie?

Arjan   But everyone told me she was dead.

Ranjit   She's not in Wolverhampton any more, so in a manner of speaking . . . she is dead.

Arjan   Does my mum know?

Ranjit   They have to bury this kind of shit. You know how it goes.

Arjan   I'll ask her.

Ranjit   Nah, don't do that, brother.

Arjan   Why not?

Ranjit *starts to laugh.*

Ranjit   You are stupid, bhenjot.

Arjan *gets up.*

Arjan   This could . . . she could be the missing piece, Ranjit, for my mum and me.

Ranjit   Nah, man . . . let a sleeping tiger rest.

Arjan   So, she's really out there, somewhere?

Ranjit   Yeah . . .

Arjan   Shit.

Ranjit   Yeah . . .

Arjan   This is a good day, Ranjit. A good day . . .

They both laugh, high from the weed.

Scene Five

Arjan *and* **Ranjit** *loiter outside the door of a non-descript council house.*

Arjan   Definitely this one?

Ranjit   Waze don't let a man down, chitterface [*bumface*].

Arjan   I didn't imagine her on a council estate.

Ranjit   She ended up with a no-good gora, ennit? Plenty of them living round here.

Ranjit *takes out a spliff. Lights it.*

Arjan   They might have bought the place. Your dad was positive about his name?

Ranjit (*consults phone*)   Jim Wilson.

Arjan   What if it's the wrong one?

Ranjit   Let's hope so. I mean look at this shithole.

Arjan (*checks phone*)   If he's kept up his subscription to the West Midlands Sales Reps Association, he must be . . . alright.

Ranjit *passes* **Arjan** *the spliff. He shakes his head.*

Ranjit   Have it, you pindoo!

Arjan *takes it. Inhales. Almost falls over.*

Arjan   What the hell is in that?

Ranjit   The real bad man shit. (*A beat.*) You know . . . if the shop gets too much for you lot, we can help.

Arjan   Thanks.

Ranjit   Could even take it off your hands.

Arjan   What?

Ranjit   When you sell it. If it makes things easier. I mean you lot can't manage the place forever.

Arjan *is really high now. He starts laughing uncontrollably.*

Ranjit   Calm down, chitterface [*bumface*].

The door opens. **Jim** *emerges. Life has not been kind to him. The three men stare at one another for a few moments.*

Jim   What do you want?

Ranjit   We're from His Majesty's Revenue and Customs.

Jim   Eh?

Arjan   We'd like to talk to your wife, Mrs Surinder Wilson.

Jim   Are you joking me?

Arjan   Sorry if we've got the wrong person.

Jim   Right person. Wrong decade. I haven't heard that name since . . . since a long time.

Arjan   But you were married? To Surinder Bains?

Jim   Sue? Tried putting a ring on her finger but . . . no . . . Any money she owes, that's down to her.

Arjan   When was the last time you saw her?

Jim   Like I said, a long time . . . Sue . . . my dark lady . . . my valiant Sue . . . I was never . . . enough for her.

Ranjit   You got any idea where she is?

Jim (*shakes head*)   If you find her, tell her . . . tell her, it's okay. I'm okay. And that I'm sorry . . . and I owe her a couple of packets of Benson and Hedges.

He shuts the door. Silence.

Arjan   Fuck.

Ranjit   Shit.

Arjan   Fuck.

Ranjit   I know . . . she smokes!

Arjan   What do we do now?

Ranjit   Only one thing to do.

Scene Six

Loud, raucous musical montage of **Arjan** *and* **Ranjit** *doing drugs. Dancing in a club. Having drinks with two young women.*

Ending up in a flat with the women.

Ranjit *is passed out in a corner. One of the young women is playing on a PlayStation.*

The other woman and **Arjan** *start to kiss.*

Scene Seven

Arjan *and* **Claire** *sit at a table with a couple of drinks.*

Claire   How much stuff?

Arjan   About two hundred quid's worth. I chased them down the road, but these kids are used to running. So they're fast.

Claire   Sounds like youngsters being stupid.

Arjan   Even if they don't steal anything, there's an edge in the air. As if we've taken something that doesn't belong to us, because we're not from here.

Claire   You are from here.

Arjan   It's like they believe we've got more than we deserve. I get up at 4.30 every morning!

Claire   Most of those kids are likely to be living in poverty.

Arjan   I know that. And I get that all this . . . fucking skullduggery isn't fair.

Claire   Fucking skullduggery?

Arjan   Yeah.

Claire   Have you turned . . . gangster now?

Arjan   This isn't London, living cheek by jowl with refugees and billionaires. Here, everyone's in their tribes. I have to face the shit on a daily basis. And I'm sick of being a target. The police said they'd come and take a statement. They didn't show up for ten days. (*A beat.*) I don't mean to go on, I'm a bit . . .

Claire   Forget it.

Arjan   I've got something to say.

Claire   I've got something to tell you too.

Arjan   Can I go first? Please.

Claire   Okay.

Arjan   This is hard. Might be time . . . for us to take a break.

Claire (*A beat*)   I thought you wanted to get married.

Arjan   I did. I do . . . but I can't.

Claire   Why?

Arjan   Because . . . of everything.

Claire   Spell it out.

Arjan   We fell in love when I was a metropolitan creative director, but now I'm a provincial shopkeeper. (*A beat.*) You know my dad grew up in India. Not like my mum . . .

Claire   Yes . . .

Arjan   So when he spoke Punjabi, it was proper, desi. When he said 'Kiddha Putth', he made these sounds that she can't make. That I can't make. And now he's gone, it feels like those sounds, my dad's sounds are lost. I'll never hear them again.

Claire   This is grief, Arj. Normal grief.

He shakes his head.

Arjan   You don't know what 'Kiddha' means. Or why Tupperware is more important than central heating. I used to think Asian men who dated white women and then went on to marry Asian women were cowards who caved under emotional pressure, but now I think they give in because it's . . . impossible. Because you can't understand how responsible I feel for my family . . . my mum . . . more responsible than I am for my own life. It's like I've been programmed and I can't fathom another way to be. I thought love conquered all but now I'm not sure . . . how to make sense of anything . . . The problem is, ultimately, you're white. And I'm brown.

Claire   Is that how you see me . . . as someone who's just . . . white?

Arjan   No . . . I dunno . . .

Claire   Do you honestly believe what you've said?

Arjan   I had to speak it out loud.

Claire   Whatever you're feeling . . .

Arjan (*interrupts*)   I had sex with someone. I was drunk. I barely remember.

Claire   No . . .

Arjan   Yes.

Stunned **Claire** *gets up from the table.*

Arjan   I'm sorry. About everything.

Silence.

What . . . what did you want to tell me?

Claire (*A beat*)   I found your aunt.

Arjan *is speechless.*

Claire   You kept looking for Surinder Bains but you said Jim Wilson called her Sue so I looked for Sue Bains. She runs a hotel. I'll send you her details.

She starts to go.

Arjan   Don't go.

Claire   You can't expect me to stay.

Arjan   Say something.

Claire *comes back to the table, picks up her drink and chucks it in his face.*

Scene Eight

Arjan *sits in a lobby.* **Surinder** *enters. She is older, weathered but chic.*

Surinder   Hello, I'm Sue.

Arjan   Hi.

Surinder   You've seen the brochure?

Arjan   Yes.

Surinder   I can show you around the space and we can go through some options.

He stares at her.

Is that alright?

Arjan   We were getting married. But now . . . it's complicated.

Surinder   Well . . . are you still planning to book your reception?

Arjan   My name's Arjan Banga. I'm the son of Tanvir Singh Banga and Kamaljit Kaur Bains.

Long silence.

Surinder   Why have you come here?

Arjan   I wanted to see you.

Surinder   So . . . Kamaljit and Tanvir got together?

Arjan   Yeah.

Surinder   What about my mum?

Arjan   Oh . . . er . . . Bibi died years ago.

Surinder   How?

Arjan   I was only a kid. Cancer, I'm pretty sure it was . . . cancer.

Surinder *takes this in.*

Surinder   Was she in hospital?

Arjan   No, she was at home. Mum and Dad looked after her.

Surinder   That's good. I'm glad.

Arjan   She had dementia towards the end.

Surinder   My mum?

Arjan *nods.*

Surinder   But she was sharp, quick . . . she could add up a basket of shopping in her head in five seconds . . . my mum . . . she kept us all alive . . .

Arjan   I realise this is a lot to take in . . .

Surinder   Yeah.

Arjan   At least you . . . followed your heart.

Surinder   How do you know what I did? (*A beat.*) Sorry, it's . . . I never imagined a moment like this . . .

Arjan   I went to see Jim Wilson.

Surinder   Who told you about Jim?

Arjan   Uncle. Mr Dhanda.

Surinder   Still going strong, is he?

Arjan   Practically runs the town. (*A beat.*) Jim said to say he's okay and that he owes you some cigarettes.

Surinder *half laughs.*

Arjan   Do you have a family? Kids?

Surinder   No. (*A beat.*) Does Kamaljit know you're here?

Arjan   She doesn't. But she'll be delighted. I'm sure she will.

Surinder   And . . . how's your dad?

Arjan (*A beat*)   There's a lot to catch up on.

Scene Nine

Bains' *living area.* **Kamaljit** *is tidying up, she clatters around loudly.* **Arjan** *tries to help.*

Kamaljit   Get out of my way.

Arjan   You've already dusted the place to death.

Kamaljit   If she runs a hotel, she's used to inspecting rooms.

Arjan   I think she just wants to see you.

Kamaljit   How do you know?

She stops. Takes a breath.

Kamaljit   The dhal and the lamb's cooked. The samosch are on the side. Did you get the imli chutney?

Arjan   Yes.

Kamaljit   What if she doesn't eat Indian food anymore?

Arjan   She must do.

Kamaljit   She's been around goreh for years.

Arjan   They eat more Indian food than Indians.

He checks his phone.

Kamaljit   You should call that Claire.

Arjan   She's blocked me.

Kamaljit   So block her back.

Arjan   It doesn't work like that . . . I mean she won't know . . . doesn't matter . . .

Kamaljit   Maybe it's better in the long run.

Arjan   I still love her, Mum.

Kamaljit   Love doesn't last. Look at your Masi and that chocolate salesman.

Arjan   You loved Dad.

Kamaljit   No I didn't.

Arjan   You had a love marriage!

Kamaljit   Yes, but after a few years he started getting on my nerves. (*A beat.*) I liked him. And I respected him, but you only love someone at the start. Did you put the ketchup out?

Arjan   What?

Kamaljit   In case she doesn't want chutney.

Arjan   I'll get some from the stock room.

Kamaljit   I told you to do it before.

Arjan   Don't you want her here?

Kamaljit   You should have asked me.

Arjan   I thought it'd make you happy.

Kamaljit   Since the day I was born everyone thinks they know what's best for me.

Arjan   I can tell her not to come.

Kamaljit   Her train must be here by now.

Arjan   I'll text her, we can meet for a coffee instead.

Kamaljit   I've made the dhal and the lamb now! And who's going to eat the fifty rotis I've made?

Arjan   Why did you make so many?

Kamaljit   I don't know!

She sits down.

Go and find the ketchup. And check the chah.

Arjan *leaves.* **Kamaljit** *breathes deeply. Takes out a small book, covers her head. Puts her hands together, quietly says a prayer in Punjabi. As she is praying,* **Surinder** *enters. She stares at her sister.* **Kamaljit** *senses eyes on her, she notices* **Surinder***, closes the book, takes her chooni off, stands.*

Surinder   Arjan said to come through.

Silence. **Surinder** *indicates the prayer book.*

Are you . . . religious?

Kamaljit   Yeah . . . no . . . I mean I don't know . . . I made samoseh.

Surinder   Oh.

Kamaljit   You still eat them?

Surinder (*nods*)   I'm sorry about Tanvir.

Kamaljit   Yeah . . . well . . . one day he was alive and now . . . he's not.

Surinder   You look the same.

Kamaljit   No, I don't. You don't. When did you cut your hair?

Surinder   Years ago.

Kamaljit   Sit down.

Surinder   I'm fine.

Kamaljit   Sit!

Surinder *sits.*

Kamaljit   So you got the train?

Surinder   Yeah.

Kamaljit   Haven't you got a car?

Surinder   Yes, but it was easier.

Kamaljit   Is there a toilet on the train?

Surinder   What?

Kamaljit   It's a long journey, isn't it?

Surinder   Yeah, but I didn't use it.

Kamaljit   Do you need the toilet now?

Surinder   No.

Kamaljit   You should go.

Surinder   I'm okay.

Kamaljit   You don't want to your bladder to burst.

Arjan *comes in.*

Arjan   Everything alright?

Kamaljit   Yes.

Surinder   Yes.

Kamaljit   Get the samoseh. Don't forget the imli. And the ketchup and the chah.

He exits.

He had a girlfriend.

Surinder   Right.

Kamaljit   She was okay. White girl.

Surinder   Right.

Kamaljit   You've probably got a lot in common.

Arjan *comes back in with a tray.*

Kamaljit   She blocked him.

Surinder   Who?

Kamaljit   Claire.

Arjan   We split up.

Kamaljit   Her decision.

Surinder   That's a shame.

Kamaljit   And we sent him to private school. We couldn't afford it, but we sent him.

Arjan   I didn't want to go.

Kamaljit   Tanvir said he was destined for medicine. He wasn't.

Arjan   I hated science. You know I hated science.

Kamaljit   He used to steal cigarettes from the shop and sell them at break time. They phoned us and we had to go and sit in front of the headmaster. In his actual office!

Surinder   Oh . . .

Arjan   I paid all the money back.

Kamaljit   Eventually.

Arjan   I was only twelve.

Kamaljit   Imagine if we'd done that.

Surinder   We'd get battered.

Kamaljit   We'd be dead. (*A beat.*) And I couldn't have any more kids after him because my uterus was upside down. Or back to front. Or something.

Arjan   It's called a retroverted uterus, Mum.

Kamaljit   Now, he's a doctor! (*A beat. To* **Surinder**.) Have a samosa.

Surinder *picks one up. Takes a bite. Eats. Puts the samosa down.*

Kamaljit   Too much chilli for you?

Surinder   No. It just . . .

Kamaljit   What?

Surinder   Tastes like Mum's.

She gets emotional. **Kamaljit** *turns to* **Arjan**.

Kamaljit   Tissues.

He leaves. **Surinder** *composes herself.*

Surinder   Are you angry with me?

Kamaljit When the internet came out . . . have you got the internet?

Surinder Yeah.

Kamaljit I thought you might send an email . . . but you didn't.

Surinder I couldn't find a way . . . to start . . . of saying what I wanted. (*A beat.*) Was Mum alright?

Kamaljit No. (*A beat.*) But we were here so after a bit, she managed.

Surinder Tell me . . . things.

Kamaljit Things?

Surinder About her. Your wedding. When Arjan was little . . .

Kamaljit *gets up.*

Kamaljit I can't . . . colour it all in, not just like that . . .

Surinder No.

Kamaljit No.

Surinder Why did you tell Arjan I died in a car crash?

Kamaljit Because it was . . . it felt like . . . you did.

Surinder You knew I was out there.

Kamaljit At the beginning, we used to get called names, laughed at . . . a hundred stares fixing on us at the Gurdwara. And we took it. Mum and me, we had to tolerate the sky caving in on us . . . I didn't want them to make my son feel shame.

Surinder You shouldn't have lied.

Kamaljit You left me! Do you think it was easy to watch our mum turn into a raving bag of bones? Sitting there . . . rattling. She turned old so fast. (*A beat.*) And I didn't even know if you were still breathing. No sister by my side on my wedding day. No Daddy. No Daddy. (*A beat*.) I made up a story so I could miss you and . . . cry. (*A beat*.) But you know what, Surinder . . . I never once stopped praying . . .

Surinder   Did Mum talk about me?

Kamaljit (*A beat*)   Me and Tanvir used to.

Surinder   I asked about Mum.

Kamaljit   She never spoke your name.

Surinder   Not even to curse me?

Silence. **Surinder** *tries to cover her upset.*

Daddy shouldn't have brought us here.

Kamaljit   You can't blame Daddy.

Surinder   I'm trying to understand how they expected us to live . . .

Kamaljit   Daddy got called a Paki every single day of his life. But when he rested his head on his pillow at night, he did it smiling because he knew he was building something. Him and Mum might have got most of it wrong, but they tried. You can't say they didn't try.

Surinder   Yeah.

Kamaljit   You were his boy. His good boy. (*A beat*.) The years that have gone are gone.

Surinder   Some bits have been ugly, Kamaljit, really ugly.

Arjan *brings the tissues.*

Surinder   I'm sorry for . . .

Kamaljit   Shut up! What did you do wrong? Nothing! You're my baby sister.

She starts to sing the chorus from the theme from The Monkees. She points to a box on the side.

Kamaljit (*to* **Arjan**)   Give me that.

He hands it to her. She opens it, gives it to **Surinder** *who takes out an envelope.*

Kamaljit   Open it.

Surinder *opens it, takes out a slip. Reads.*

Surinder   Biology A, Chemistry A, English Language A, English Literature A, French A, History B, Latin A, Mathematics A, Physics A . . .

Arjan *picks up the slip.*

Arjan   You were brilliant.

Kamaljit   Never mind about the B.

Arjan   Why didn't you go to university?

Arjan *gets a text. Leaves.*

Kamaljit   How did you get rich?

Surinder   Me?

Kamaljit   You're not poor. You don't look poor.

Surinder   I worked for a landlord. Learned the property business. Bought a place and then another and then another . . .

Arjan *leads* **Dhanda** *and* **Ranjit** *in.*

Dhanda   Oh my God. Oh my God. It is you.

Surinder   Sat siri akal.

Dhanda   Surinder Kaur. Welcome home.

He holds out his arms. She doesn't move.

Dhanda   She is the exact image of her mum. (*A beat. To* **Surinder**.) You remember your mum?

Surinder   Yes.

Dhanda   Bhanji was a great lady!

Surinder   She was.

Kamaljit   Have a samosa, Uncle.

Dhanda   No, no, no. We are merely passing.

He nudges **Ranjit** *who is holding a box of Indian sweets.*

Ranjit   Bought you some barfi.

Surinder   Thanks.

Dhanda   This is a blessed day. Your mum would be happy to see her daughters reunited. No need to worry about your sister. We are here.

Ranjit   Course we are.

Kamaljit   Uncle's been very kind.

Dhanda   Kamaljit and Tanvir were left alone you see. They needed support.

Surinder   Right.

Dhanda   You should come and see my shop. Buy Express! I have a butcher's counter and a Slush Puppie machine. (*A beat.*) Plus I sell chips, hot from the microwave.

Kamaljit   That's nice isn't it, Surinder?

Surinder   Yeah.

Dhanda   You look like you have had a good life, Surinder Kaur. That is what is important. To have a good life. No matter what has passed, we do not break from each other. Even when we don't see each other's faces. You are our girl. No matter what.

Ranjit (*to* **Arjan**)   You coming out later, chitterface [*bumface*]?

Arjan   I'll message you.

Dhanda   We will leave you in peace.

Kamaljit   See you at the Gurdwara, Uncle.

Dhanda *and* **Ranjit** *head out.*

Surinder   How do you manage the shop on your own?

Kamaljit   Arjan's here. When he leaves, I'll sell the place.

Arjan   What?

Kamaljit   You told me to live in a cottage and potter in the garden.

Arjan   You said you'd never sell.

Kamaljit   Uncle thinks it might be a sensible idea.

Surinder   Uncle.

Arjan   You're not selling the shop, Mum.

Kamaljit   Are you going to stack toilet rolls for the rest of your life?

Arjan   If I have to.

Kamaljit *gets up.*

Kamaljit   I'll check the lamb.

She leaves.

Arjan   Must be strange . . . to be here, I mean.

Surinder (*A beat*)   This place was always . . . full of people . . . every day there was some . . . tamasha . . . And your dad, your dad was the best person . . .

She half laughs.

Surinder   She must be lost without him.

Arjan   We both have been.

Surinder   Perhaps . . . if you like . . . I could help out, now and again . . . if that's useful.

Arjan   You've got your own life.

Surinder   I'm okay. I enjoy myself.

Arjan   What happened to you?

Surinder   Doesn't matter . . .

Surinder *gets up walks around the space, looks around, soaking it all in. Half laughs to herself, almost in disbelief.*

Scene Ten

Bains' *living area.* **Ranjit** *is checking a light fitting, he holds a screwdriver. There is a cup of tea on the side and a plate of biscuits.* **Ranjit** *stands back, admires his handiwork. Picks up the tea.* **Kamaljit** *enters, sets up an ironing board.*

Ranjit   Done. You won't get any more flickering now.

Kamaljit   You didn't have to, beta.

Ranjit   That light'll give you headaches. Can't have you ending up down the doctor's, Auntie.

Kamaljit   You are a sweet boy. How are your little ones?

Ranjit   Pair of wrestlers. Always trying to bite each other's ears off and kick the other's private parts. Nina usually breaks it up.

Kamaljit   You are lucky to have Nina.

Ranjit   Arjan still hasn't found his Juliet?

Kamaljit   I thought he had but . . .

Ranjit   He wants to hurry up. You must be desperate for grandkids.

Kamaljit   I'm okay.

Ranjit   My two keep my mum and dad alive. They know there's a new generation rising up to take their name. Show the world what that name means. You've worked hard all these years, Auntie, time to put your feet up.

Kamaljit   Your daddy keeps busy.

Ranjit   He can't stop work. Jat blood running through his veins.

Kamaljit   Yes.

Ranjit   Although, he's been . . . under the weather recently. Mum reckons he should go to the GP.

Kamaljit   He does eat a lot of sugar.

Ranjit   It's not his sugar.

Kamaljit   What is it then?

Ranjit   It's you.

He takes a biscuit, eats it.

Kamaljit   Me?

Ranjit   These are tasty. Really very tasty.

Kamaljit   What do you mean about your dad?

Ranjit   He's worried about you. (*A beat.*) Your sister's been down the shop a few times, asking questions.

Kamaljit   Surinder's been helping out . . .

Ranjit   Helping?

Kamaljit   She's here most weekends, getting the place into shape. Your dad's very successful, she's probably looking for inspiration.

Ranjit   Did you know she's applied for an alcohol licence?

Kamaljit   Yes, she said if I want to sell, I'll get a better price.

Ranjit   Are you selling?

Kamaljit   I still haven't decided.

Ranjit   So if you keep hold of the shop, you'll stock alcohol?

Kamaljit   Is that a problem?

Ranjit   If you live on Whittington Road and you fancy a bottle of cider, you walk up Bridge Street onto Victoria Road, into our shop. But if you lot are selling that same bottle of cider, you might as well turn off Whittington, go left on Garwood Avenue, through the alley and there's you lot.

Kamaljit   We're much smaller than you.

Ranjit   My dad's a decent man.

Kamaljit   Yes.

Ranjit   This whole thing, the way she's gone about it . . . it's . . . hurt his feelings.

Kamaljit   We don't want to do that.

Ranjit (*A beat*)   How much do you know about her?

Kamaljit   She's . . . my sister.

Ranjit   You know me. And my dad. He's like your dad. We've got your interests at heart. You understand, don't you?

Kamaljit *nods.*

Ranjit   You came to the hospital the day I was born.

Kamaljit   Ranjit . . .

Ranjit   It's not about money. This is not about money. I'd give my life for you, Auntie. And this is what you're doing.

Kamaljit   I'm not doing anything.

Ranjit   I get it, it's her. She's not one of us. We've got on fine all these years. Where was she?

Kamaljit   It's complicated . . .

Ranjit   You don't know, do you?

Silence.

Ranjit   Do you trust her? Trust her in your bones?

Surinder *and* **Arjan** *bustle in, laughing. They see* **Ranjit**. *Take off their jackets.*

Surinder   Hello.

Ranjit   Alright.

Arjan   What are you doing here?

Ranjit *indicates the light.*

Ranjit   Loose wire.

Surinder   I could have fixed that.

Ranjit   Should be down to Arj. You wanna look after your mum, chitterface.

Arjan   I do.

Ranjit   Only messing. We going Red Lion tonight?

Arjan   I don't think so.

Surinder   We're getting a takeaway if you'd like to join us.

Ranjit   Nah, man, can't be eating outside food. Nina'll have my roti ready. Come for one.

Arjan   Not tonight, thanks.

Surinder   I'll order. What do you want, Kamaljit?

Ranjit (*to* **Arjan**)   You're coming!

Kamaljit   Dhal and roti.

Surinder   You have that every day.

Kamaljit   Because I like it.

Ranjit *gets* **Arjan**'s *jacket.*

Ranjit   Put this on.

Surinder   I'm having masala fish and a pizza.

Arjan   Ranjit . . .

Kamaljit   That doesn't go.

Surinder   It's what I fancy.

Ranjit   Hurry up . . .

Arjan   No.

Ranjit   Arj!

Surinder   He said no.

Arjan   I can speak for myself, Masi.

Ranjit   You sure about that brother? Looks like this one's running things round here.

Surinder   This one?

Ranjit   You know what I mean. Arj knows.

Arjan   I'll see you another time, Ranjit.

Ranjit   You chucking me out?

Arjan   Thanks for fixing the light.

Ranjit   I'm your brother . . .

Arjan   No, you're not.

Ranjit   Who was looking after your mum and dad when you were drinking soya lattes in London with your goree?

Kamaljit   Ranjit . . .

Ranjit   This woman you haven't seen for years, turns up and takes over. She's not even married.

Arjan   Shut your mouth.

Ranjit   She wants the shop for herself.

Surinder   Not that it's any of your business but I'm here for my sister. I've got my own money.

Ranjit   You want more. I know a dirty gold digger when I see one. Behsharam [*Shameless*].

Suddenly **Arjan** *punches* **Ranjit** *in the face. Loud music plays and there ensues a massive, messy, ungainly fight. The men part and* **Ranjit** *is about to go for* **Arjan** *again when suddenly* **Kamaljit** *slaps* **Ranjit** *round the face. Music stops.*

Kamaljit   Go home. Tell your father, we're waiting for the licence to come through. And then I'm ordering a hundred boxes of lager, vodka and Aperol Spritz.

Ranjit   My dad'll make sure everyone in the Gurdwara knows about this.

Kamaljit   Tell him not to bother, I'll WhatsApp the ladies myself.

Ranjit *starts to leave.*

Kamaljit   This was my daddy's shop when your father was a penniless pindoo off the boat. And now it's mine. And my sister's. And we'll do whatever we like with it.

Ranjit *leaves.* **Kamaljit** *turns to the others.*

Kamaljit   What are you having?

Surinder   What?

Kamaljit   To eat!

Surinder   I already said . . . pizza and fish . . .

Kamaljit   Arjan?

Arjan   Er . . . pizza.

Kamaljit   Right. (*A beat.*) I'm going to have butter chicken. A large portion.

Surinder   Eh?

Kamaljit   With the dhal.

Scene Eleven

The shop. The place has been transformed. Eye-catching displays and a flashy newspaper rack. **Surinder** *unpacks boxes of crisps.* **Claire** *stands nearby, awkwardly sipping a cup of tea. There are a couple of bin bags in front of the counter.* **Claire** *looks around in admiration.*

Claire   You've got a real talent for décor. Your sister must be pleased she found you.

Surinder   Thanks to you. I'd like to take her to Paris or New York for a weekend but she reckons she can see abroad on the telly. (*A beat.*) How come you're still wearing your engagement ring?

Claire   Think I'm just . . . used to it.

Surinder   I had wedding jewellery . . . from my parents. It was meant to give me a decent start.

Claire   Where is it?

Surinder   Lost. (*A beat.*) Do you still like him?

Claire   No.

Surinder   I know that feeling. Once the hate stops . . . make sure you get on with it.

Claire   What?

Surinder   Whatever it is you want.

Arjan *brings in a couple of boxes.*

Arjan   I didn't realise I had so much stuff at your flat.

Claire   Not any more.

Arjan   You kept my old art. I'd forgotten about some of these pictures.

Claire   I almost gave them to the Scouts.

Arjan   The Scouts?

Claire   They were building one of their bonfires . . . but . . . well . . . they are yours.

Arjan   Thank you.

Claire *takes a sheet of paper from her bag. Gives it to him.*

Arjan   I remember when we found the venue. We were so excited . . .

Surinder   Are you getting the deposit back?

Claire   No. (*A beat.*) I need to make a move.

He signs the paper.

Arjan   That's it then.

Surinder *picks up the empty crisp boxes. Exits.*

Claire   Bye, Arj.

Arjan   Claire . . . wait . . .

Claire (*interrupts*)   I slept with my ex-boyfriend.

Arjan   What?

Claire   Ben.

Arjan   That solicitor fuck?

Claire   Actually, he's a barrister now. (*A beat.*) I didn't intend to. But . . .

Arjan   Revenge?

Claire   Perhaps. I don't know . . .

She heads out just as **Surinder** *comes back in with another box of goods. She starts unpacking.*

Surinder   Why did you split up?

Arjan   Because she's . . . English.

Surinder   Are you serious?

Arjan   I thought life would be simpler. I mean . . . Ranjit
. . .

Surinder *makes a face.*

Arjan   . . . might be a moron, but he knows who he is.

Surinder   He stinks of skunk. And you know why he
smokes so much? Because he needs it to get through the day.

Arjan   I suppose I . . . feel guilty about wanting what I
want.

Surinder   Guilt is about the person who's feeling it. If you
enjoy wallowing, go ahead. But get your order in with Ranjit
for an eighth of weed and be ready for the Red Lion every
Saturday night.

Arjan   What about all the things they don't understand
about us?

Surinder   What about all the things we don't understand
about us?

Arjan   My mum's got so little left. She always dreamed of
me being with an Indian girl. Bride in a red lehenga. Me
riding up on a white horse . . .

Surinder   Kamaljit married her soulmate. Had you. Still
eats fish and chips on a Friday. She's lived the life of a Rani.
(*A beat.*) Your mum's gonna hate whoever you bring home.
But give her a chance and she might start to love her.

Arjan   Thing is, Masi, the truth is . . . I don't want her to
die . . .

Surinder   And you pissing on your own life is gonna stop
that?

A beat.

Kamaljit and Tanvir always had this . . . something, like my
mum and dad. Me and Jim never did. You know when
you've got it. And if you and Claire do . . . well . . . it's up to

you. (*A beat*) Why do you think they sent you to that fancy
school?

Arjan   So I could be a doctor.

Surinder   So you get a choice. My dad came here because
he needed to breathe. Because he had an imagination.
Thanks to him and your mum and dad, the sun and the
moon and the stars are at your fingertips, and if you're not
brave enough to fight for what you want . . . that would really
disappoint your mother.

Arjan   What I want most is for her to be happy.

Surinder   Making people happy's the easy way.

Arjan   What's the hard way?

Surinder   Being who you are.

She continues to unpack. From one of the boxes he brought in,
Arjan takes out a painting, beholds it.

Movement/music sequence indicating **Arjan** *coming into his own.*

Scene Twelve

A park. **Arjan** *stands opposite* **Claire***. He takes a breath.*

Arjan   So . . . what do you say?

Claire   How can I trust you? Properly trust you.

Arjan   Because I've never told you a lie.

Claire   Why should I believe this could work?

Arjan   I think . . . we've got . . . something . . . if you don't
agree, I understand . . . but I know I've got it, for you.

He approaches her.

Claire   Is she keeping the shop?

Arjan   Yeah. They're gonna run it together. Mum's planning to open a deli counter · · · oh, and she wants to sell fresh bread.

Claire   Always a winner.

Arjan   She says a loaf wrapped in brown paper and tied with string always looks fresh. Extremely fresh!

Claire   Okay.

Arjan   It's what she wants.

Claire   What do you want?

Arjan   I'd like to come home.

Claire   Yeah.

They move closer to each other.

Epilogue

Wedding Hall. Punjabi folk music plays over the following sequence which encapsulates a Sikh wedding, it should have the quality of an emotional but uplifting dance –

Milni [meeting] – **Kamaljit** *and* **Surinder** *exchange gifts – blankets and flowers – with* **Bill.**

Post ceremony – **Arjan** *and* **Claire** *sit on the floor in Indian wedding attire.* **Bill, Ranjit, Dhanda, Kamaljit** *and* **Surinder** *throw petals at them.   Then put money in their laps. Pose for photographs.*

Music fuses into a bhangra tune. **Arjan, Claire, Bill, Ranjit, Dhanda** *and* **Mrs Bains** *all dance energetically.*

They are joined by **Kamaljit** *and* **Surinder** *as young girls, dancing with carefree joy, as if they have their whole lives ahead of them.*

THE END.